Simple Sermons for a sinful age

THE "SIMPLE SERMON" SERIES BY W. HERSCHEL FORD . . .

Seven Simple Sermons on the Saviour's Last Words
Seven Simple Sermons on the Second Coming
Simple Sermons About Jesus Christ
Simple Sermons for a Sinful Age
Simple Sermons for Funeral Services
Simple Sermons for Midweek Services
Simple Sermons for Saints and Sinners
Simple Sermons for Special Days and Occasions
Simple Sermons for Sunday Evening
Simple Sermons for Sunday Morning
Simple Sermons for Time and Eternity
Simple Sermons for Times Like These
Simple Sermons for Today's World
Simple Sermons for 20th Century Christians
Simple Sermons From the Book of Acts
Simple Sermons From the Gospel of John
Simple Sermons From the Gospel of Matthew
Simple Sermons on Evangelistic Themes
Simple Sermons on Heaven, Hell and Judgment
Simple Sermons on Prayer
Simple Sermons on Prophetic Themes
Simple Sermons on Salvation and Service
Simple Sermons on Simple Themes
Simple Sermons on the Christian Life
Simple Sermons on the Great Christian Doctrines
Simple Sermons on the Old-Time Religion
Simple Sermons on the Seven Churches of Revelation
Simple Sermons on the Ten Commandments
Simple Talks for Christian Workers
Simple Sermons on Life and Living

Simple Sermons for a Sinful Age

W. Herschel Ford

ZONDERVAN PUBLISHING HOUSE
GRAND RAPIDS, MICHIGAN

SIMPLE SERMONS FOR A SINFUL AGE

Grand Rapids, Michigan

Second printing 1971
Third printing 1972

Library of Congress Catalog Card Number 77-106431

Printed in the United States of America

DEDICATION

This book is lovingly dedicated to the precious and wonderful members of the San Jose Baptist Church of Jacksonville, Florida, where I have the honor and privilege of serving as pastor

AUTHOR'S FOREWORD

Paul says in II Timothy 3:1, "This know also, that in the last days perilous times shall come."

As we study Biblical prophecy and look at the conditions existing in this world today, surely we must come to the conviction that these "perilous times" are now upon us. This is a sinful age such as mankind has never known. Personal sin, national sin, world-wide sin fill the universe today. A glance at your morning newspaper will prove this point.

In a sinful age Christ and the Gospel are the only answer. Therefore, I hope that these simple gospel sermons will help bring the answer to many people.

As I have used the material of many others in compiling these sermons, I hope that preachers and Christian workers will use these messages for the glory of God and the salvation of souls.

W. HERSCHEL FORD

6140 San Jose Boulevard
Jacksonville, Florida 32217

CONTENTS

1. The Safest Place for the Soul 11
2. The Hound of Heaven 22
3. A Message for Backsliders 32
4. Let's Dig Some New Wells 42
5. How a Christian Can Get Everything He Needs 51
6. The Way of Transgressors 61
7. I Dreamed I Was Sentenced to Die in the Electric Chair 69
8. The Three Hardest Words to Say 81
9. The Kisses of the Bible 89
10. The Assurance of Our Salvation 99
11. The Best Things in the World 109
12. The Laughter of the Bible 119

1

THE SAFEST PLACE FOR THE SOUL

II Timothy 1:12

A friend of mine told me about the death of his father. In his last minutes he called all the family to his bedside. He asked one of his sons to read the fourteenth chapter of John, then he told each one of them good-by. Then he said, "Heaven is opening up and the angels are coming down to carry me home." Oh, it's wonderful to come to the end of the way with the assurance of salvation and eternal life in your heart. And the saddest thing on earth is for one to come to that hour without God and without hope and to plunge out into a Christless eternity.

Now Paul, when he came to his last hours, had this great assurance. Second Timothy contains the last words of the great apostle. He told Timothy that he was "now ready to be offered," and that the time of his departure was at hand. He is in prison, the death sentence has already been passed upon him, and he is just waiting for the time when his soul will sail out to be with his Saviour. He looks back over his life; he remembers his experience with Christ on the Damascus road, and all that had happened since that time. Now he writes, "I know whom I have believed, and am persuaded that he is able to keep that which I have committed unto him against that day." Years before he had committed his all to Christ and he knew that he was safe in Him forever.

You can trust your money to a bank and lose it, you can trust your friend with a secret and he may betray you. But when you trust your soul to Jesus Christ it is safe forever.

I. The Joy of Knowing Jesus

"I know whom I have believed." Paul knew Jesus, not just as a historical person, but as a personal Saviour and a dearly beloved Friend. On that day when the bright light from heaven blinded him and when he heard the Saviour's voice speaking directly to him, Paul came to know that indeed Jesus was the Son of God and the Saviour of the world. And on that day Christ became Paul's Saviour.

Persecutions of all kinds had come, Paul had suffered the loss of all things, but the one great joy of his life was that he knew Christ. Now as he comes to the end of the journey, he says, "I know Him, I know Christ, God's Son. He is my Saviour and soon I shall see Him face to face."

John knew Jesus. He followed Him for three years and leaned on His bosom at the Last Supper. When he became an old man, he wrote over and over the words, "I know, I know." His heart overflowed with the assurance of his salvation and as he closes the Book of the Revelation he writes, "Even so, come, Lord Jesus."

Peter knew Jesus. Maybe he did not know Him fully on the night when he denied Him, but he came back to know Him as a man knows his best friend. He went through many fiery trials, he was often beaten and persecuted. But at the end of the way we hear him saying, "God . . . hath begotten us again unto a lively hope by the resurrection of Jesus Christ from the dead, to an inheritance incorruptible, and undefiled, and that fadeth not away, reserved in heaven for you" (I Peter 1:3, 4). Yes, Peter knew Jesus.

And we may know Him, too. We may know Him as our Saviour by repenting of our sin and putting our faith in Him. We may know Him as our Lord and Master as we obey His Word and seek to do His will. We may know Him as our Friend as we walk by His side day by day. We may know Him as our Comforter in sorrow, our Guide along the pathway of life, our Hope for time and eternity.

When Horace Bushnell was a young man he was almost an invalid. But one day he was brought face to face with the question asked by a minister, "What do you believe?" Bushnell answered, "I believe there is a difference between right and wrong." The minister then asked him to pray this prayer, "O God, if there be a God, I do believe that there is a difference between right and wrong and I want to do the right thing. If it is right to follow Christ, show me the way." Bushnell prayed this prayer from his heart and God revealed Himself to him and Bushnell was saved and later became a minister. He served God for forty-seven years in Hartford, Connecticut. He said at the close of that time, "I know Jesus Christ better than I know anyone in Hartford."

Darwin tells us of a marine flower that floats upon the surface of the water. But the roots are at the bottom of the sea, 150 feet from the surface. The violent storms come and the waves dash high, but the flower rides safely through the storm, because its roots reach deep down and grasp solid rock. And when a man knows Christ he reaches down and grasps the Rock of Ages and nothing can move him. Let the storms come, he is secure in Christ. Yes, it is a glorious thing to be able to say with Paul, "I know Christ whom I have believed."

II. The Mighty Christ

"I am persuaded that he is able," says God's great servant. Let us think of His might.

1. *He is mighty to create.* "All things were made by him; and without him was not any thing made that was made" (John 1:3). We build our houses, our skyscrapers, our automobiles, our ships, our mighty weapons of warfare. And we build all these things out of existing materials. But Jesus built the world out of nothing. He spoke, and the sun, the moon, the stars, the planets, the worlds were made.

And it is a beautiful world. I have seen Niagara Falls and I have stood on the top of Pike's Peak. I have been through Carlsbad Caverns and have gazed down into the Grand Canyon. I have watched the restless waves of the Atlantic and have ridden on the bosom of the Pacific. I have gloried in sunrises and sunsets and marveled at the beauties of the sun, the moon and the stars. I have seen the footprints of the Almighty on the Milky Way. And I have come to realize that Jesus created all these things for our pleasure. Yes, He is able to create.

2. *He is mighty to re-create.* God creates, Satan comes in to destroy, but Jesus re-creates. God made man in His own image, the devil marred that image through sin, but Christ restores the image. A child comes into the world innocent. As the child grows the devil gets in his work. Innocence is changed to guilt, the man is opposite to what the baby was. But one day Christ comes in and changes that man. He gives him a new heart, He makes him over, He transforms him from a child of Satan to a child of God. Only Christ can do that.

Some years ago I visited a rayon plant. I watched the dark skeins of thread as they were dipped into forty tanks of chemicals before they became white. But Jesus can take a sinner and dip him once in Calvary's fountain and he becomes, in God's sight, as white as snow.

Gilbert West and Lord Littleton were two brilliant skeptics of another day. They made fun of Christians and Christianity. One day they decided that in order to defeat Christianity they must explain away the resurrection and the change in Paul and his influence on history. One of them said, "I'll study the resurrection and write a treatise showing the fallacy of it." The other one said he would write about Paul. They agreed to meet several weeks later and publish their findings. On the given day they came together and Lord Littleton said, "West, what have you to say?" He replied, "I must be honest, I studied the resurrection of Christ and found it to be absolutely true. I saw myself as a sinner, I trusted Him as my Saviour and now I have peace for the first time in my life." "Thank God for that," said Littleton, "I studied the conversion and the life of Paul and, like him, I saw myself as the chief of sinners, and on my knees I became a Christian." Oh, I tell you, only Christ can take men like that and make them over into the image of God.

3. *He is mighty to comfort and inspire.* When a Christian loses a loved one he goes down into the valley, but he comes up with a light on his face and peace in his heart. Why? Because he has a Comforter.

Someone has painted a picture of Christians in the Roman Coliseum, awaiting their death at the hands of the hungry lions. They are kneeling in prayer and one of their number is leading them. The crowds in the stands are waiting with feverish expectancy, the lions are stalking toward their prey. But the faces of the Christians are alight with the glory of God and hope is filling their souls.

James, one of the disciples of Jesus, was beheaded by one of the Herods. It is said that when he was led to the execution block, his conduct was so sweet and his courage so great that his executioner repented of his sin, declared himself a Christian and died with James. He could do this because he felt beside him the presence of the mighty Christ.

Think of the missionaries who have given up all for Christ; think of the millions of Christians who have been faithful in giving their time, their money, their talents, their service, to Christ. Think of the preachers and teachers and other Christian servants who go on and on, often in hard places, serving their Master because they are inspired by the mighty Christ.

4. *He is mighty in history.* Someone has well said that history is simply "His-story." The world has never been the same since Jesus lived. Even the calendar divided at the Bethlehem manger. Time would fail us to tell of His influence in the world, but as one studies history he can see the footprints of the King all along the way, shaping the destinies of men and nations.

III. The Keeping Christ

Paul says, "He is able to keep that which I have committed unto him."

1. *He keeps the soul.* Paul knew the value of his soul. He knew it would live forever, so he said, "I give my soul to thee, O Christ, keep it for me forever." And he was assured that Christ would do just that.

A great fire raged on Broadway in New York, completely destroying a large business concern. However, the safe in the office was unharmed. The company that made the safe wanted to advertise this fact, so they set it out on the sidewalk and placed a sign over it, saying, "This safe stood the test of the fire. Both the safe and its contents were saved." In like manner the Lord Jesus could say, "No man who has put his trust in Me has ever been lost, and none ever shall be. I will keep the soul safe throughout the endless ages of eternity."

2. *He keeps our good deeds.* One day a woman, in love and gratitude, broke open an alabaster box of very precious ointment and poured it on the head of Jesus as He sat at the dinner table. He was so moved by this good deed, by this expression of love, that He complimented the woman, and said that in the years to come her gift would be spoken of everywhere as a memorial to her. He never forgets what we do for Him. The aroma of our good deeds will fill the halls of heaven, because He remembers that what we do for Him here and now will bless us throughout eternity.

3. *He keeps our departed loved ones.* Paul had said "good-by" to many whom he loved and had worked with. He had seen them slip away beyond the shadows. But he knew that they were safe with Christ. In writing to the Thessalonians he spoke of them and of how they would be kept safe in Christ until one day we meet them again. Then, in a burst of hallelujah he says, "so shall we ever be with the Lord."

We are not to look into the ground for our departed loved ones and friends who trusted the Saviour. They are with the Lord and He will keep them safe unto the perfect day and beyond. Their frail bodies rest in the grave, but when He comes in the air He will raise those bodies, make them perfect like His own, join them to their spirits and take them to be with Him forever.

Some years ago I conducted the funeral of a fine Christian doctor. His last case had been that of a twelve-year old girl who had been injured and who recovered under his skillful ministry of medicine. When she stood by the doctor's casket, she pointed to certain flowers and said, "I don't want to cry. As I look at these flowers I realize that they will go to sleep, but they will awake in the morning. It is the same way with the doctor." Yes, Jesus has our loved ones in His care and He will keep them safe forever.

4. *He keeps the future.* It has been well said that we do not know what the future holds, but we know who holds the future. We often look down over the years and wonder what life will be like ten or fifteen years from now. But it is best for us not to know what is coming in this world. We look forward, however, with hope and joy, toward that which is coming when life is done. We don't know what the world is coming to, but we know Who is coming to the world. And we can know that we can trust Him for the rest of life's journey and for the endless years of eternity.

I know not what the future hath
Of marvel or surprise,
Assured alone that life and death
His mercy underlies.

Yet in the maddening maze of things
And tossed by storms and flood,
To one fixed trust my spirit clings,
I know that God is good.

And if my heart and flesh are weak
To bear an untried pain,
The bruised reed He will not break,
But strengthen and sustain.

And so beside the Silent Sea
I wait the muffled oar;
No harm from Him can come to me
On ocean or on shore.

I know not where His islands lift
Their fronded palms in air,
I only know I cannot drift
Beyond His love and care.
— *John Greenleaf Whittier*

IV. The Day of Reckoning

Paul tells us that God will keep that which He has committed unto Him "against that day." What kind of day will that be?

1. *That day will be a day of judgment.* The real Christian is not afraid to face that day. He has committed his all to the mighty Christ and he has no fear of condemnation. "There is therefore now no condemnation to them which are in Christ Jesus, who walk not after the flesh, but after the spirit" (Romans 8:1).

In the palace of Versailles there is a statue of Napoleon in exile on the island of St. Helena. There is something sad about his face. His mouth is compressed, his chin is lowered, he stares gloomily into the distance. He is looking back at Waterloo, where he lost everything. The battle there was lost because of a three hour delay on the part of his reinforcements. Delay is always costly. And there are some who are passing Christ by today, postponing their decision for Him. They may delay too long, and from the halls of hell they will look back and cry, "The summer is ended, the harvest is past, and I am lost, lost forever." But the Christian has no fear of the day of judgment. Let the rivers of death flood over his soul — he is safe in Christ.

2. *It will be a day of accounting.* The Bible over and over rings out with the truth that one day every soul must stand in judgment before the Great Judge. The Christian will stand before the Judgment Seat of Christ to give an account of his works for Christ and to receive His reward.

The unsaved man will stand at the Great White Throne Judgment to have the sentence of eternal death passed upon him.

What will Jesus say to you in that day? Will He say, "Well done, thou good and faithful servant"? Or will He say, "Depart from Me into the everlasting fires, I never knew you"? It will be a day either of blessed assurance or a day of desperate despair.

3. *That day will be the glorious crowning day of Christ.* In the day of Great Britain's glory, the king would come to Westminster Abbey to be crowned, and all the lesser rulers of the Empire would come to the coronation, robed in resplendent royal regalia. The king would be crowned with great pomp and ceremony. Then all the other rulers would come and lay their crowns at his feet.

And in that glorious day when Jesus Christ is crowned as King of kings and Lord of lords, we shall bow humbly before Him and lay our crowns and our all at His blessed feet.

A young man went away to college. A few months later his mother visited the campus. He showed her around the buildings and proudly introduced her to some of his professors. Then she said, "I'd like to see your room." He took her over to the dormitory and into his room. As she looked around she saw some lewd pictures on the wall, but she was wise enough not to say a word. But after she got home she sent him two presents – one for himself and one for his room. When he opened the package marked for his room, he found a beautiful picture of the head of Christ. When she visited him in the spring, he again took her into his room. All the obscene pictures had been taken down and the picture of Christ had the central place in the room.

"Where are the other pictures?", his mother asked him. "Oh," he said, "I took them down and destroyed them. I saw that they did not fit in with Him." He had cast out the evil and had crowned Christ, giving Him the first place. That's exactly what we ought to do. We should throw out of our lives and hearts all those things that would displease Him and we should crown Him as the Lord of our lives.

Like Paul did in the long ago, let us commit our all to Him until that blessed day when we see Him face to face and He is crowned King of kings and Lord of lords.

2

THE HOUND OF HEAVEN

John 11:28

Francis Thompson wrote a poem called *The Hound of Heaven.* In referring to God in this manner he was not trying to be irreverent. He was simply saying that wherever he went, God followed him, to save and bless him. He was right, for God is like that. He seeks men in order to save them and then He does everything in His power to help them.

Now in the little village of Bethany there was a home that Jesus loved. He loved that home because of His three wonderful friends who lived there, Mary, Martha and Lazarus. When the world was pressing in on Him, He loved to go there and find peace and rest. It was not a large home, and it was not richly furnished, but Jesus loved it because love was there. This little family loved Jesus with all their hearts. Oh, for more homes like that today!

There came a time when Jesus was away on a preaching tour, and while he was away Lazarus died. Jesus did not return immediately, so his sisters went ahead with the funeral. As they reached home after the service, from broken hearts they said, "If Jesus had been here our brother would not have died." Sometimes when sorrow comes we think God has forgotten us, but that is never true. His eye is on the sparrow and He cares for you and me. The Christian life is never one without trouble, but He is with us in every dark valley. He has not promised skies always blue, but He has promised to be with us to the end of the way.

Four days after the funeral Jesus did come back and Martha went out to meet Him, while Mary sat in the house, brokenhearted. It was then that Jesus spoke those immortal words about the future life, "I am the resurrection and the life," He said, "He that believeth in me, though he were dead, yet shall he live. And whosoever liveth and believeth in me shall never die." Receiving comfort from His words Martha went to Mary and said, "The Master is come, and calleth for thee." You know what happened next. They all went out to the cemetery and Jesus called Lazarus back from the grave and restored him to his happy sisters.

As Jesus called Mary, so does He call people today. He wants to save them and bless them and give them a home in heaven. God is always running after sinners. Even as far back as our first parents who lived in the Garden of Eden, God was calling, for after Adam and Eve had sinned we hear God in the garden in the cool of the evening, calling out, "Adam, where art thou?" And He has been calling ever since. Now how does God call people?

I. He Calls Them Through The Bible

All the way through the Bible we hear God calling, calling, calling. His favorite word seems to be the word "Come."

Hear Him as He speaks in Isaiah 1:18, "Come now, and let us reason together, saith the LORD; though your sins be as scarlet, they shall be as white as snow; though they be red like crimson, they shall be as wool." Hear Him calling again in Isaiah 55:1, "Ho, every one that thirsteth, come ye to the waters, and he that hath no money: come ye, buy, and eat; yea, come, buy wine and milk without money and without price."

Again we hear His call in Matthew 11:28, "Come unto me, all ye that labour and are heavy laden, and I will give you rest." And in John 6:37 He says, "All that the Father giveth me shall come to me; and him that cometh to me I will in no wise cast out." Then when He is about to close the Book, we hear Him saying in Revelation 22:17, "And the Spirit and the bride say, Come. And let him that heareth say, Come. And let him that is athirst come. And whosoever will, let him take the water of life freely."

Do you say, "God has never called me? If He ever calls me I will come to Him, but not before"? God has called you. All through His Word He has called you. Every invitation of the Bible is a special invitation to you, written on holy pages and sealed with the blood of His dear Son.

When you meet God some day you can't say, "I didn't know the way out of my sin, I didn't know the way to heaven." For He will say, "I gave you a Guidebook, I filled its pages with earnest calls. I wanted you to come, but you refused my invitations. You are without excuse."

II. He Calls Them Through Christians

I have heard lost men say, "I wish those church people would leave me alone about my religion." But we can't do it. God has commanded us to "persuade men." We must listen to Him. This is every Christian's business. We have found Christ and know the joys to be found in Him. We have tasted of the Lord and found that He is sweeter than the honey in the comb. We must tell others about Him, that they, too, might enjoy this sweetness.

Jesus told of a man who made a great supper. Then he sent his servants out to say, "Come, for all things are now ready." The invited guests refused to come, so the invitation was extended over and over again. Finally when the guests refused to come the master said, "Go out into the highways and hedges, and compel them to come in, that my house may be filled" (Luke 14:23). We who are Christians are God's servants. It is our obligation to give out His invitation to men to come to Christ. We simply can't, we simply must not be quiet.

But someone will say, "You often do more harm than good when you do personal work." If your life is not what it ought to be, that is true. If there is sin in your life, you should be quiet. But if your life is right, if you are following the Holy Spirit's guidance, you can go in the name of Jesus and He'll bless your efforts. He invites men to come to Him, He commands us to go for Him.

An evangelist tells the story of a certain unsaved man who came to hear him preach in a revival. This man's best friend was converted one night and in his newfound joy he went to the unsaved man and said, "God has saved me and I am anxious about you. I am praying for you; I want to see you saved." The unsaved man said, "I'm a grown man, I know what I am doing. I came to enjoy the sermon. If you bother me again I'll never come back." A few nights later the new Christian came to his friend in the church and said, "I know you asked me not to speak to you again, but I am so burdened for your soul that I cannot find peace until you are saved." The man flared up in anger and said,

"I told you not to come to me again like this. Now I'll never come back. I hope you are satisfied." Then he walked quickly out of the church.

The unsaved man went home and went to bed, but he could not sleep. Conviction for sin seized him and brought tears to his eyes. "What a fool I am," he said, "my best friend loves me and wants to see me saved and I insulted him. Now no one else will come to me and I'll go to hell." The burden became so heavy that he got out of bed, fell upon his knees and cried out to God for forgiveness. Of course God saved him, for did He not say, "Him that cometh to me I will in no wise cast out"? (John 6:37) The preacher had announced a sunrise prayer meeting at the church and when the janitor arrived at 5 A.M. he found this man waiting on the church steps, ready to make his unashamed confession of Christ as Lord and Saviour. Yes, God often calls through the voice and heart of a Christian.

Some years ago I conducted a revival in Black Mountain, N.C. One night a boy came down the aisle to give his heart to the Saviour. He told the pastor and me of his decision. We told him to take a seat on the front pew, but instead he went back into the congregation. He stood up on a seat and began to talk to his father about the Lord. Soon the father came down the aisle with the boy to make his confession of Christ.

Not only Christians, but Christian churches call men to Christ. Hundreds of lost people pass by the church building every day and the building itself is always quietly saying, "You need the Christ that I represent."

Oh, lost friend, your Christian friend knows two things. He knows about the horrors of hell and a Christless eternity. And he knows the joy of sins forgiven and wants to share that joy with you. Do not resist his earnest appeal, do not resist the voice of God as He speaks through some loved one or friend.

III. He Calls Them Through His Goodness

"The goodness of God leadeth thee to repentance" (Romans 2:4). If any sensible man will just stop and think, he will have to say, "God has been good to me and I ought to serve Him." Do you think that you are doing well in your job because of your own wisdom and strength? Do you think you received that promotion because of your intelligence? No, God is responsible for it all. He gives you the strength and wisdom for every task and He could easily take it all away in a second's time. A man is a base ingrate not to realize that God is responsible for everything he has and does.

Every meal that you eat speaks of God's goodness. Every night that you sleep, every paycheck that you draw, every time you look into the face of a loved one, all these come because of God's goodness. Anything good that comes your way should make you say, "God has been good to me."

When a boy loves a girl he does everything in his power to prove it. He sends her flowers and says, "You are more lovely than any flower." He sends her candy and says, "You are sweeter than the sweetest morsel." He sends her a book and says, "You are more interesting than any volume." But no lovesick swain ever sought to show his love as much as God seeks to show His love for lost sinners.

IV. He Calls Them Through Trouble

It is easy to see how God calls in other ways, but it is hard to believe that He calls men through trouble, also. Still there are some who will not read the Bible, who will not heed the pleas of a friend, who will not recognize the goodness of God. So in a last desperate effort God sends trouble to bring men to His side. You may say that this is a harsh way for Him to deal with men, but it is certainly not as bad as leaving them alone and letting them go to hell.

There are some eyes that will never see Jesus unless those eyes are washed with tears. There are some ears that will never hear the voice of God as long as those ears are filled with the things of this world. Some men love their business so much that they forget God, so God must smite that business to make them see their need of Him. Often God takes away some precious thing in order to get us to remember Him and give our hearts to Him.

A little baby died, and as the baby's father stood by the freshly-made grave, he said to the pastor, "Preacher, that's God's call for me to be a Christian." And often it is just that.

Joab had a barley field which he loved. Now Absalom wanted to send a message to David by Joab, so he sent his servant to tell Joab to come to him. Joab refused to come. Absalom sent his servants the second time and still he refused to come. So Absalom told his servants to set fire to Joab's barley field. This calamity brought Joab running to Absalom. It took trouble to make Joab move. God calls men and they refuse. He calls again and again and they still refuse. Then God sends trouble upon them and they can no longer ignore Him. They must come to Him.

Some seminary students were preaching in a jail and there they found a woman who had become a Christian. She said to them, "I thank God that I was sent to jail. Outside I never went to church, I never listened to a preacher, I never gave God a thought. But," she said, "I got into trouble and was put in prison. My heart was broken, all the future looked black. But here in prison I heard the Gospel and have been saved. I would have gone to hell if I had not gotten in trouble and been brought to jail."

Often in Oriental countries the shepherd has a difficult time getting the sheep to cross over some stream. So he takes a baby lamb in his arms and carries it across the stream. The mother sheep runs up and down on the other side of the stream, but soon, because of her love for her lamb, she plunges into the stream and crosses over. And often, in His love and wisdom, God must take our little ones in His arms in order to get us to follow them to Christ and heaven.

Some years ago I was having dinner with a preacher friend in Atlanta, Georgia. A phone call came asking him if he could conduct a funeral for a four-year old boy the next day. He could not accept the assignment but asked me if I would go in his place. I consented to do this. When I went to the funeral parlor to learn all the circumstances I found that the little boy had been killed in an accident on one of the city streets. He had been playing with some marbles, when one of them rolled out into the street. He rushed out to get the marble and a streetcar ran over him and crushed him to death. The motorman had not seen him in time to stop the car.

It became my sad duty to try to comfort the little boy's parents. I learned that his mother was devoted to the little fellow, but that she was not a Christian. In my funeral message I tried to tell them that maybe God had taken the little one that the older ones might follow. And I used this illustration of the shepherd taking the lamb across the stream. Then we went to the cemetery for the burial and when we turned away from the little grave, the young mother said to me, "I believe I know why God allowed my little boy to be taken. I have not been a Christian, but,

God helping me, I will go to church next Sunday, give my heart to Christ and live for Him all of my days. I do want to see my little boy again." And who knows but that God was using this tragic accident to bring another soul into the kingdom of heaven?

Shakespeare said, "Sweet are the uses of adversity." The sweetest use of trouble is to bring us to Jesus. And God not only uses trouble to bring the lost to Himself, but often to bring the backsliding Christian back to His side and service.

In Proverbs 29:1, we read, "He, that being often reproved hardeneth his neck, shall suddenly be destroyed, and that without remedy." What is God saying here? He is saying, "I'll call and call you and if you refuse to hear My call I will have no mercy on you."

Dr. Jesse Hendley tells of something that happened when he was holding a tent meeting in Atlanta. A certain woman and her daughter-in-law came to the meeting and were gloriously saved. Then one night the elder woman said to the preacher, "I am going to bring my son to the service tomorrow night and I want you to pray for him to be saved." The young man did come the next night and heard Dr. Hendley pour out his soul for the lost. During the invitation he saw the Holy Spirit shake the young man like the wind shakes the leaves on a tree, but the young man made no response. The next morning the mother called the preacher on the phone and weepingly said, "My son was killed on the job this morning." Apparently God called for the last time, he refused the call and was taken away.

A boy in Scotland was wild and wayward, living in sin and breaking his mother's heart. One night he became intoxicated and lost consciousness. When he woke up he found himself on a freighter, bound for Australia. He worked for a while in the gold mines of Australia and then he staked out a claim of his own. Several months later he struck it rich. His first thought was of his mother and how he had treated her. He said to himself, "I'll go home and buy her the finest house in town. I'll hire servants to wait upon her, and I'll take care of her and never cause her another minute's worry as long as she lives."

He sailed for home and when he landed he hurried to his mother's house. The door was locked so he knocked and knocked and called out his mother's name, but there was no response. A neighbor saw him there and came over and led him out to the little cemetery. He saw there a new grave and a little sign with his mother's name on it. He fell across the grave and sobbed over and over, "Mother, I loved you, I did, I did." And the neighbor softly said, "Jack, you told her too late."

There is One who loves you more than any mother ever loved a son. He died for you and wants to fill your life with eternal blessings. Don't wait too long to return that love; don't wait too late to give yourself to Jesus.

"The Master is come, and calleth for thee." Will you heed that call?

3

A MESSAGE FOR BACKSLIDERS

Mark 16:7

All of us are interested in Simon Peter because he is so human, he is so much like the rest of us. He had his ups and downs, he was sometimes good and sometimes bad, he was often on the mountaintop and often in the valley. When we look at his failures, remembering how close he was to Jesus, we become discouraged and feel there is no hope for us. But when we look at his successes, although he was an ignorant, unlettered man, we feel there is some hope for ourselves.

I like Peter's enthusiasm. He was always bubbling over. When the Master suggested any course of action he was always for it and wanted to get going at once. God needs men of enthusiasm today. If Martin Luther had not been enthusiastic we would not have had the Reformation. Moody said, "If I must choose between the man who had knowledge without zeal and the man who had zeal without knowledge, I would take the zealous man every time." A man may not know everything, but if he is zealous about the things that he does know, he can do great things for God.

Then I like Peter's bravery. We don't think he is so brave as he quails before two maids and a man and denies any knowledge of or connection with Jesus. But I would have you to remember that he did follow Christ into the presence of the Saviour's enemies, while all the other disciples except John fled in fear.

Now look at this scene. The crucifixion is over, the rocks have ceased their throbbing and the three crosses are empty. The world goes on as usual for most people, but it has changed altogether for one small group. They are the disciples of Christ. They had followed Jesus, expecting great things for themselves. They expected Him to set up an earthly kingdom and give them the prominent places in that kingdom. But now He is dead; He can do nothing for them. They gather in the Upper Room and sob out their sorrow on each other's shoulder.

But Peter is not with them. He has denied Jesus, his best Friend. Now he is out yonder somewhere, weeping his heart out. As the disciples think of him and his denial, they say, "Yes, that's just like Peter, always saying and doing the wrong thing at the wrong time." But Peter is lonely and sad and he says to himself, "I'll go and find the other disciples, maybe they can give me a word of encouragement." So he goes to join the others, but they have no word of comfort to give him. They are just a bit angry that he would dare to join them after his denial of the Saviour.

But suddenly a voice is heard on the stairway, "Where are the disciples of Jesus?" And then a woman bursts into the room. It is Mary. She shouts, "I have seen Jesus. He is alive; He is risen just as He said He would. He sent me to tell you to meet Him at the old trysting place in Galilee." Immediately all of the disciples except Peter spring up and rush out of the door. But Peter lingers behind, "He didn't mean me. I am no longer one of His disciples, for I denied

Him." "Oh," said Mary, "He especially mentioned you. He said, 'Tell my disciples, and Peter.' Yours is the only name He mentioned. Of course He meant you."

Now wasn't it wonderful of Jesus to remember Peter. But He always does that. A man said to a dear, old, saint, "Wasn't it wonderful for Jesus to die for sinners like you and me?" And she answered, "No, that was just like Jesus." And it was just like Him to remember poor brokenhearted Peter. So Peter ran to meet Jesus. His sin was forgiven and and he was given a new hope and a new message. He became the greatest preacher of his day.

Peter was a backslider. What is a backslider? It is not simply a man who joined the church, then went back into sin. It is a man who has been genuinely saved, but who has drifted back into the world. However the true Christian is not happy there, away from fellowship with Christ. Some of you have been saved; you have eaten at the Master's table, but you are out of fellowship with Him today. Surely you are not satisfied, surely you miss that sweet communion with Him. You long for a better life. Well, Jesus sends you a special message today. "Come back," He pleads, "come back to your old place of joy and power and peace. Come back to your first love."

I. The Causes of Backsliding

1. *You haven't gone deep enough with God.* A little boy fell out of his bed. When his mother put him back in the bed, she asked him why he fell out and he replied, "I guess I went to sleep too close to where I got in the bed." Christians are like that. They get into the kingdom through faith in Christ, but then they go to sleep. They live always in the ankle depths of the Christian life, when they should be going deeper and deeper every day.

Look at the door of a great temple. You see the door and that's all; you must go inside to see the real beauty of the temple. And you don't see all the beauties nor enjoy all the blessings of the Christian life if you don't go farther than just the door. Oh, it's important to make a living, to get a good education, to become a good citizen. But it is more important to grow in grace, to go deeper with God. So leave the shallow depths, lest you be swept out into sin.

2. *You have been disobedient to the call of God.* Jonah had a call from God and he ran from it. Then he found nothing but trouble and misery until he turned back to God's will for his life. God may not have called you to be a preacher or a missionary or to occupy some prominent position, but He may be calling you to some humble place of service, to sing in the choir, to teach a class, to tithe, to visit that neighbor in the name of Christ.

Not to obey His call is to slip farther and farther away from Him, but there is peace and power, happiness and usefulness, in an obedient life.

3. *You may have been hurt by trouble and sorrow.* Trouble and sorrow ought to bring people closer to Christ, but often it has just the opposite effect on them. Some years ago I held a meeting in a small North Carolina town. There was no one present to play the organ, so just the piano was used. I asked the pastor where their regular organist was, and he said, "She lost her son some weeks ago and we have not been able to get her back to church." She was pursuing the wrong course. She was turning her back on the very thing that could have brought comfort to her. Some people do backslide and turn away from God when sorrow comes.

Todd Hall was a detective in Baltimore. He attended a

Moody meeting, was gloriously converted and became a preacher of the Gospel. His daughter, whom he greatly loved, became ill and lay dying. When the doctor gave him this news, he said, "God gave her to me, He saved her, and now I'll give her back to Him." After that the people said that Todd Hall preached with a power and pathos he had never had before. Oh, if sorrow and trouble have weaned you away from God, He is sweetly calling you today to return to Him and the peace and joy He alone can give you.

4. *You have gotten in with the wrong crowd.* Peter's place was right by the Lord Jesus, but he was outside, warming his hands at the enemy's fire. And many Christians backslide because they leave the company of dedicated Christians and go out to associate with the world. If the best Christian gets on the level with the world, he will go down. You can't run with the worldly crowd and stay close to Christ.

It is true that Jesus associated with publicans and sinners, but He never got down on their level. He went with them to help them, to love them, to lift them up, to save them. That should be the only reason for our going out to them. But when you lower yourself to the level of the world, when you do things the wordling does and go to the places he frequents, you are bound to backslide.

5. *You have a fear of what others will say.* The Bible says that "the fear of man bringeth a snare" (Proverbs 29: 25). A man becomes a Christian and really wants to live for Christ. But a testing time comes. Shall he follow Christ or the crowd? He is afraid of what the crowd will say, so he stifles his convictions, goes with the crowd and thus denies Christ. No wonder he backslides.

6. *You have neglected your Christian duties.* Once you

were regular in your church attendance, your prayer life, your Bible study, your tithing. But you have allowed other things to come between you and these simple Christian duties. Of course you have backslidden. Your theme song is now, "Where is the joy that once I knew when first I met the Lord?" You had it, but you lost it, you lost it in neglect. Go back and find it where you lost it. Go back to an active and faithful Christian life.

Some years ago I was in a small town for a revival and a visit was made to a family a block away from the church, to try to interest them in transferring their church membership from a church in a distant part of the state to this church nearby. The father in the family said, "We like the church, we like the preacher, we like the people, but we've never moved our membership because we don't know how long we're going to be here." "How long have you lived here in this place and near this church?", he was asked. And he answered, "We've lived here twenty years, but we don't know whether we'll be here permanently or not." Think of it! Twenty years wasted that might have been given to God, twenty years when their children were coming up and needed the ministry of that church. Oh, how unwise some people can be!

7. *You let some secret sin creep in.* A person's hair doesn't turn gray overnight; it is a slow process. And sin doesn't usually overcome us in a day; it is a gradual process. We turn the wrong way one day, we get closer to sin the next day. Finally we have embraced it and in so doing we blot out the face of God like a cloud blots out the sun.

We have to live in the world, but we don't have to be of the world. Have you ever noticed a beautiful lily growing in the swamp? It lifts up its head in all the beauty and whiteness of that glorious flower, but its roots are in the black mud of the swamp. It is not content to stay in the mud; it rises above it. And Christians are to be like that. They must live and walk in a filthy and sinful world, but with God's help they are to rise up above the world and its sin.

A man tells about climbing a high mountain in the Rockies. Finally he was up so high that the storm clouds were below him and the bright sun above him. Then he saw a great eagle as he fought his way up through the clouds and toward the sun. That's what Christians are to do. They are to fight their way above the world and toward the Sun of Righteousness. When secret sin slips in we always backslide.

II. Consequences of Backsliding

1. *Doubts come.* When we backslide we get far from God and we begin to wonder if we have been saved. We begin to doubt some of the great truths of the Bible. This is the devil's work. He gets an opening into our hearts and lives and soon our minds are filled with doubts. We need to stay close to Jesus, then the doubts will fly and we can say with Paul, "I know whom I have believed, and am persuaded that he is able to keep that which I have committed unto him against that day" (II Timothy 1:12).

2. *Joy is lost.* There is no real joy in a backslider's heart. He once knew that joy but now that he has lost it, he cannot be happy.

David was a happy man in the Lord, a man who could write the wonderful twenty-third Psalm. But there came a day when he fell into gross sin, breaking at least four of God's Ten Commandments at one time. After this sin there followed a time of misery and uncertainty for him. He spoke about it in Psalm 32:3, 4, "When I kept silence, my bones waxed old through my roaring all the day long. For day and night thy hand was heavy upon me; my moisture is turned into the drought of summer."

Then there came the day when God's prophet, Nathan, confronted him with his sin. "Thou art the man," thundered out Nathan. David shrank before the accusation but quickly confessed his sin to God. In his confession he cried out, "Restore unto me the joy of thy salvation" (Psalm 51: 12). And God heard that prayer and soon floods of joy were filling David's soul again and he was testifying, "Blessed is he whose transgression is forgiven, whose sin is covered" (Psalm 32:1).

Have you lost that joy? Then you can find it again as sure as David found it. Confess your sin to God, repent of it and forsake it and God will forgive and restore.

3. *The soul shrivels up.* If a man is not fed he will starve; if the soul does not feed upon the Bread of Life it will grow lean. If the flower is not watered it dies; if the soul does not feed upon the Water of Life it shrinks up. Don't you want your soul to grow? Don't you want some spiritual power? Don't you want to be of service to God and man? Then leave your backslidings and feed your soul upon the things of God.

4. *Jesus is cheated.* He gave His best for you. He came all the way from heaven's glory to Calvary's gory for you. He deserves your best. But the backslider is cheating Him. His influence counts for the world and not for Christ. One man lives close to Christ and has a positive influence for Him. Sinners look at him and are impressed by his life. They are brought to see their need of a Saviour. But the man who is a backslider has no influence for Christ. Instead he is cheating Him.

Recently a Japanese ship was sunk in the Panama Canal and scores of ships could not make passage through the canal for many hours because of it. The backslider is like that. Souls are held back from Christ because of the blockade he forms. No one looks at him and says, "That man's life makes me see the reality of Christianity and my need of a Saviour." Just the opposite is true.

III. The Cure for Backsliding

We have diagnosed the case and thought of the disease. Is there any cure? Yes, there certainly is. Three simple steps become the remedy.

1. *Break off all that is wrong in your life.* Sit down alone and make a thorough self-examination. Probe every deed and word and thought. The Holy Spirit will guide you; He will show you the things that ought not to be in your life.

Then forsake these things; tear them out by the roots. Say to them, "I am through with you forever, from now on I'll walk and talk with Jesus."

2. *Pray for forgiveness.* The publican prayed, "God be merciful to me a sinner." That has been called the sinner's prayer; it can also be the backslider's prayer.

Yes, storm the gates of heaven and ask for God's forgiveness. And as sure as the sun shines and the mountains stand and the rivers run and the leaves fall and human hearts love, just so sure will God forgive you. He is waiting for you to come back to Him, waiting for you to confess your sins, waiting with open arms to welcome you and forgive you.

3. *Come back to the side and service of Christ.* We are told by jewel experts that pearls can become sick and lose their luster. In order to restore that luster the pearls are returned to their native waters and soon the color is restored. The soul of a backslider is a sick soul. It needs to

be restored to its natural position, right by the side of Christ and in the midst of good service for Him.

Let's think again of Simon Peter. We hear him weeping his heart out and saying, "I can never serve Jesus again. Now I am worth nothing to Him and never shall be." But look at that great congregation on the day of Pentecost. Look at those three thousand souls pressing into the kingdom of heaven. Who is that great preacher who conducted the service? Why, it's Simon Peter. He was worth something to Jesus after all, simply because he repented of his sin and came back to the side and service of Jesus.

Maybe you think you are not worth anything to Christ, because you have been living a backslidden life. But come back to Him. Tell Him all about it, trust Him for forgiveness, love Him and serve Him. He'll make life over for you. His message to you is the same as His message to Simon Peter. "Return unto Me," He says. "Leave those things that have separated us and I will forgive you and give you a new happiness and a new joy."

On the long journeys through the desert caravans often run out of water. Then they will send men out at different intervals of time to seek fresh water. When the first man finds an oasis and water he cries out to the next man behind him, "Come." And he cries out the same word to the next man behind him, and he to the next until the welcome message reaches the caravan.

So from the fountain of life I hear Jesus calling, "Come, come, come." He says, "Come and drink of all the blessings I have for my faithful children. Come unto Me and drink." Backslider, will you do it?

4

LET'S DIG SOME NEW WELLS

Genesis 26:17-25

Today when we want a supply of water we just turn on a faucet and the water comes out. But it was different years ago. We went to a well, let the bucket down into its depths, and drew it up full of cool, sparkling water. In the small towns the town well was the center of the community. The people met there, drew water for their horses and for their homes, and passed around the news of the town. This means of communication took the place of a newspaper. The poet was stirring up nostalgic emotions when he sang of "The old oaken bucket that hung in the well." Some of the old timers today, caught in the trappings of a furious modern life, would often like to go back to those simple days.

Now Isaac felt that way. His people were nomads, moving from place to place. They never built permanent homes, and they lived in tents. As they traveled they found the wells that their father Abraham had dug many years before. Memories flooded their hearts as they found these old wells. But they were filled with the debris of many years, so they dug the wells again and drank the sweet waters from them.

But in this message I want us to think about some spiritual wells. We drank deeply of these wells when we were first converted. But the years have gone by and these wells have become choked with sin and worldliness and neglect and indifference. So we need to get busy today and dig some of these wells anew.

I. We Need to Dig Anew the Well of Prayer

Years ago I saw a sermon which had the title, "The Sin of a Prayerless Life." Yes, it is a sin when we accept all of God's blessings and never stop to thank Him for them. Do you need anything? The Bible says, "My God shall supply all your need according to his riches in glory by Christ Jesus" (Philippians 4:19). But the supply is dependent upon prayer. We must ask God for what we need.

The place of prayer is the place not only of provision, but it is also the place of power. Moses found power on the mountaintop with God. Paul found power in the loneliness of the desert. Jesus found power in the Garden of Gethsemane. Do you have a place of prayer where you can find provision and power?

Go to Niagara Falls and you will see millions of gallons of water roaring over the falls every second. That water creates great power, power that lights up large cities and turns the wheels of commerce and industry. But go to a quiet room where you see a Christian on his knees, and you will realize that here is a power greater than a thousand Niagaras.

What has prayer done? It has divided the seas and rolled up the flowing rivers. It has made the rocks to gush in the wilderness. It has quenched the flames of fiery furnaces. It has muzzled lions and offset the poison of vipers. It has conquered devils and commanded angels. It has recalled souls from death. It has tamed the sinful passions of men. It has beaten and routed and destroyed armies of atheists.

During World War II someone asked the question, "Has Christianity failed?" And the answer came back, "No, but all else has failed." We have the same situation today. We have tried money, we have tried pleasure and social prestige, we have tried drink and dissipation and all else. But these things have been found empty; they fail to bring us any joy. Yet God and Christ and Christianity are still the same, and we reach them through the power of prayer.

George Adam Smith was a dynamic preacher of another day. He went to Switzerland and climbed the highest mountain there that a tourist could climb. When he reached the top he was about to leap to his feet in enthusiasm. But the guide pulled him down and said, "On your knees in a place like this." And today as we face the future with all of its uncertainty, we would be wise to say, "On our knees at a time like this." Yes, we need to pray, we need to dig anew the old clogged-up well of prayer.

II. We Need to Dig Anew the Well of Bible Study

This well is choked quicker than the well of prayer, because it takes more time. We can breathe a prayer any time; it takes hours to make a study of God's Word. The Bible is the best seller in the world, but one of the least-read books on earth. Every home has one or more Bibles, but many of them are never opened. Yet we miss the best of the world's literature and the greatest of divine wisdom when we neglect the Bible.

The ignorance of the Bible today is most appalling. Some time ago the Minister of Education for France was making a speech as a tribute to the war dead of his country. He quoted Paul's familiar words, "O death, where is thy sting?

O grave, where is thy victory?" And he attributed this quotation to Hall Caine, the English author. Some years ago Roger Babson published a leaflet with the title, "Essentials of Business Success." The leaflet contained absolutely nothing but a reprint of the Ten Commandments. Some time later a western manufacturer wrote to Mr. Babson and said, "Those are the finest rules I ever saw. Where did you get them?"

1. *In the Bible we find bread for our hungry souls.* During the Civil War a soldier lay in the hospital, sick and depressed. Then his father came to see him and said, "I've brought you a loaf of your mother's bread." Soon the soldier was on the mend. Oh, sin-sick souls, oh, struggling, unhappy Christians, you need the Bread from heaven, you need God's Word.

2. *In the Bible we find tonic for our sick hearts.* A shepherd in Scotland would call his sheep and they would always follow him. Someone asked, "Will they follow a stranger?" And the shepherd answered, "Only if they are sick." Do you know why so many church members follow false doctrines and false religions? It is because they are sick spiritually, it is because they have not taken the tonic of God's Word. The one who follows the Bible never follows error.

A certain woman joined the church where I was pastor. For a time she was faithful in her attendance, but after a while she stopped coming altogether. I called on her and urged her to return to church, but my pleas were in vain. Some months later I met her and she told me that she had joined an off-brand church which I shall not mention. It is a church which denies most of the cardinal doctrines of the Bible. If she had been faithful, if she had followed His Word, she never would have gone so far astray.

3. *In the Bible we find peace for our troubled spirits.* A neurotic New York City woman went to a Christian doctor for an examination. He could find nothing wrong with her, but he said, "This is my prescription for your ills. Go home and read your Bible an hour a day for a month, then come back to me." This seemed to be a silly thing to her, but she said, "There's no harm in it, so I'll try it." At the end of the month she came back to the doctor, glowing with health and happiness, and saying, "I feel wonderful. Your prescription was the right one." And the Christian doctor replied, "If I omit my daily Bible reading, I lose my greatest source of strength."

4. *In the Bible we meet Jesus face to face.* And that's the best part of it all. Begin in Genesis and walk through the pages of the Old Testament and you'll never find the words "Jesus Christ." But in every book you come face to face with Him. He is in every type, every sacrifice, every prophecy. Then when you come to the New Testament there He is, the very heart of it. If you want to meet Jesus face to face, follow Him through the pages of the Bible.

III. We Need to Dig Anew the Well of Faithful Church Attendance

We have seen the pictures of the Pilgrims, trudging their way to church through the deep snow. It was cold, there were dangers on every hand, and the father carried his gun on his shoulder. But they felt the need of a fresh touch with God, so they made their way to God's house. We need that touch with God just as much now, if not more, than they did. When a Christian absents himself constantly from the services of the church, he may not go down into sin, but certainly something good goes out of him.

I am thinking of a church member I had in the days long

gone. He was one of the most faithful members of that particular church. He was not only present at every service, but he also invited and influenced many others to attend. He put his church first in his life. If there was a choice to be made between a service at his church and some other meeting, he chose the church. Then this man, who owned a store, bought a store in another city. He soon found it necessary, as he thought, to drive to this other city over the weekend to look after his interests there. Of course this meant that his church attendance began to go down, although he would sometimes drive furiously on Sunday afternoon to get back home for church on Sunday night. But soon his entire interests were shifted from his church to his business. Things did not go well with him and the last time I saw that poor man, he was in a prison cell. Yes, it certainly is true that something goes out of a man when he neglects his church attendance.

Strength and power are found in God's house as in no other place. Get into your church and become a faithful member. Give your best to its work and take all the church has to offer you. You'll be a stronger person because of it. The church means little to some people, because they don't give it a chance to help them. They are not faithful.

IV. We Need to Dig Anew the Well of Moral Righteousness

We need to learn to say again, "This is right and this is wrong." Some years ago I traded my old car in on a new one. The speedometer showed that it had been driven 48,000 miles. Some days later a man who was considering the matter of buying my old car from the dealer, called me to get some further information about the car. He told me that the speedometer showed 32,000 miles. This meant simply that the dealer had taken off one-third of the mileage to get a better price for the car. I was told that this is done often. But surely such practice is wrong. The few extra dollars are not worth the sacrifice of Christian principles.

V. We Need to Dig Anew the Well of Service

Here is where the wells turn into rivers. Isaiah said that God's man would be "like rivers of water in a dry place" (Isaiah 32:2). It is wonderful what one consecrated man can do. Christianity is a giving religion, "God so loved . . . that he gave." Christ emptied Himself of His glory, then He came down and literally gave Himself away. That's what He wants us to do. He wants us to empty our lives of self so that He can fill us with the Holy Spirit. Then we are ready to give ourselves to the world.

Two little lakes lay in the bright sunshine on top of a mountain. One lake said to the other, "I am going down into the world. The fields down there are parched and the wheels of industry are still. Maybe I can be of some help." But the other lake said, "Not me, I'm comfortable here, I'm going to stay here." So the first lake burst its bounds, flowed down the mountainside and into a needy world. Because of it the fields were watered and became productive and the wheels of industry began to turn. Then the sun drank up the waters into a cloud and the wind blew that cloud right over the mountain top. The cloud then poured the water back into the lakebed from where it had come. The lake looked over toward the other lake and, behold, it was gone. It had dried up as it rested there on the mountain top. One lake lived because it gave, the other one died because it refused to give. This is a parable that fits human life. The man who gives of himself is really living, the man who refuses to give of himself is only existing.

It is said that above a chemist's table you can find magnets with tools hung upon them. The chemist says that if he allows the magnets to lie idle on the table they will lose their power. So he gives these magnets something to do and they grow stronger every day. That's the way God makes magnets out of men. When they loaf they lose their power. When they stay busy they develop a power that can lift men toward Christ. The man who serves God develops and grows in grace.

VI. We Need to Dig Anew the Well of Power

There was as much nuclear power in the world a thousand years ago as there is today, but men were limited in their use of it by their ignorance. And there is as much spiritual power in the world today as there was on the day of Pentecost. But men are limited in spiritual power because they lack knowledge of God and close communication with Him. If men knew God better and lived closer to Him they would have more spiritual power.

But you can't expect to have spiritual power if you leave out of your life these things I've mentioned, namely prayer, Bible study, faithful church attendance, moral righteousness and service. Spiritual power never comes free; you must pay dearly for it.

Two men were looking at Niagara Falls and one of them said, "There is the greatest undeveloped source of power in America." The other man replied, "No, the greatest undeveloped source of power is in the souls of men. Just connect them vitally with God and they could turn the world upside down." Dwight L. Moody was told, "The world has yet to see what God can do with one man who is fully surrendered to Him." Moody said, "I'll be that man." And God took this humble, uneducated man and used him to turn two continents toward heaven.

So, as God's messenger, I would call you back to the old paths. I call you out of worldliness and neglect and sin and indifference into a life of prayer and Bible study, of faithful church attendance, of moral righteousness, of service and spiritual power.

A tightrope walker was challenged to walk on a rope across Niagara Falls from the American side to the Canadian side. He accepted the challenge and the rope was stretched above the falls. But first, before he began his walk, he placed a large star on the Canadian side above the rope. Then, keeping his eye on the star, he began his walk. As he walked out over the falls the people gasped and some fainted. But the man went on and on, never looking down but always at the star. And soon he was safe on the other side. He kept his eye on the star and reached his goal.

Friends, you and I have a Star to guide us. Jesus is that Star. Keep your eye on Him and not on the world. Then one day the prize will be yours!

5

HOW A CHRISTIAN CAN GET EVERYTHING HE NEEDS

Matthew 6:33

This wonderful text, given to us by Jesus Himself, tells us that if we seek first the kingdom of God and His righteousness, all these things will be added to us. All of what things? Well, Jesus had just been talking about food and raiment, so He meant that all the material things we needed would be added to us.

What does the phrase, "Seek ye first the kingdom of God and his righteousness" mean? It means that God is to be put first in all things. It means that we are to live rightly before God. It means that we must apply all of His principles and teachings to our daily living. It means that we must have His Spirit in all things.

To put it more simply this means that, first, we are to be all that Christians should be; second, that we are to do all that Christians ought to do; third, that then God will add unto us all needed things. This is the way for a Christian to get all that he needs. Let us see how we can measure up to the standard set forth in this text, and then let us see what God has promised us.

I. We Must Have Christ's Spirit

We know what it means to have a sweet spirit or a stubborn spirit or a gentle spirit. But what does it mean to have the spirit of Christ?

1. *It is the spirit of love and forgiveness.* Look what Judas did to Jesus. He had walked with Jesus for three years. Jesus had shared everything good with him. Yet when the chance came for Judas to sell Jesus out, he sold him for thirty pieces of silver. Then he led the mob to the Garden where Jesus was, planted on His cheek the kiss of betrayal, and turned Him over to His enemies. Did Jesus hate him for doing this? No, He called him "friend." And if Judas had fallen on his knees and confessed his sin and asked for forgiveness, Jesus would have taken him in His arms and forgiven him. That was the spirit of Jesus, the kind of a spirit we must have.

Look at what Peter did. Jesus was his best Friend. He had given Peter the highest place among the disciples, and had favored him in a hundred ways. When Jesus then stated that He was going to Jerusalem where they would slay Him, Peter leaped up and said, "Lord, I'll die for You. They'll have to kill me before they get to You." Then in the hour when Jesus needed him, Peter lined up with His enemies. He cursed and said, "I never knew the Man." But did Jesus hate him? No, when Jesus was led out of that court He gave Peter a look of love and forgiveness. Then later, when they met on the beach, Jesus said, "Peter, do you love Me?" That was the spirit of Jesus. Do you have it?

In a mission school in China years ago, it was the custom for the teacher to give a prize at the end of the week to the boy who stood at the head of the spelling line. On the last day of one week a little heathen boy stood at the head, and a little Christian boy stood in second place. A word was given to the heathen boy and he missed it. He began to sob, for he knew he would lose the prize. Then the Christian boy spelled the word correctly and the teacher told him to move up to the head of the line. But the little fellow just smiled and shook his head. Then another boy said, "Teacher, he's a Christian, he wants to be like Jesus." The teacher was amazed, for she knew the boy had been a Christian only two weeks. So she asked him why he didn't want to go to the head of the line and gain the prize. The boy answered, "Me not want to make the heart of Au Fon sad." That's the right spirit, the Christian spirit. The real Christian never wants to hurt anyone, even his worst enemy How do you measure up?

II. We Must Have Christ's Attitude Toward Others

Oh, that we might take His spirit into every relationship of life – personal, national, international. How much better off this world would be, how much happier we would all be!

Take the capital and labor problem. If the capitalist and the labor leader would sit down together and make every decision under the guidance of the Holy Spirit and in prayer and in the spirit of Christ, there would be no strikes and no labor problems. The capitalist and the labor leader would look on each other as brothers and try to negotiate in the spirit of that relationship and in the spirit of Christ. The capitalist would consider the needs of the laboring man and the labor leader would consider the limitations of the capitalist. There have really been some instances where this spirit prevailed in certain firms and the results were marvelous, both for capital and labor.

Then there is the race problem. It, too, could be solved,

not by extreme measures on both sides, but in the spirit of Christ. The white man ought to treat the black man as if he were Christ wrapped up in a black skin, and the black man ought to treat the white man as if he were Christ wrapped up in a white skin. Then there would be no trouble between the races.

God made both races. He loves them both, and Christ died for them both. And when white men and black men recognize each other as brothers under the skin and treat each other as Jesus would, then our problems would be solved. We must not fight for a superiority of one race over another, but for the equality of all men before God and in our hearts and minds.

Then take the matter of the differences that we have often with other people. These differences will come up, but they ought to be short-lived among Christians. When some difference comes up because of some hasty word or thoughtless deed, the two parties ought soon to sit down together and settle their differences in the spirit of Jesus. They ought to treat each other as if the other party were Christ Himself. Then our differences would melt and we would be a thousand times happier. What kind of a Christian do you want to be, one in name only or one who lives like Jesus? We must have His attitude toward others if we are to be the best Christians.

The Bible says, "Let not the sun go down upon your wrath" (Ephesians 4:26). The sun of life will soon go down, death is coming. Do you want to meet Jesus with something standing between you and someone else? Yes, we need to have His attitude toward others.

III. We Must Have His Attitude Toward The Church

Our attitude toward the Church is not to be a critical,

faultfinding attitude, but one of love and devotion and loyalty. Let me say three things about His relationship to the Church.

1. *He founded the Church.* There are many wonderful institutions in the world, each of them founded by fine men, but the most glorious institution on earth is the Church and it was founded by Jesus Christ Himself. In fact, it is the only institution that can make that claim.

If you are faithful to other institutions and organizations and not to the Church, you are on the wrong track. Jesus is devoted to the Church. He wants to see it prosper and you can help in reaching that goal.

2. *He loved the Church.* I believe it is still the dearest and nearest thing to His heart on the earth. If we criticize it, if we neglect it, if we fail to support it, this proves that we don't love it. And surely Christians ought to love the thing that Jesus loves.

3. *He gave Himself for it.* "Christ also loved the church and gave Himself for it" (Ephesians 5:25). Yes, He created it, He loved it, He gave Himself for it. Would you give yourself for it? Are you giving it your time, your tithe, your talent?

IV. We Must Have His Attitude Toward God

What attitude did Jesus have toward God the Father? It was an attitude of great reverence and great love. He sought to please Him in all things. He talked everything over with Him.

In John 8:29 He said, "I do always those things that please him." And God could say, "This is my beloved Son, in whom I am well pleased" (Matthew 3:17). Can God say that He is well pleased with you? What is your attitude toward Him?

V. We Must Love Jesus Supremely

Christianity is not simply a matter of being baptized, or joining the church, it is falling in love with Jesus. In sadness of heart and out of many years of pastoral experience, I must say that Jesus Christ doesn't mean much to the average Christian. He thinks in terms of belonging to a church or going through some ritual, and not in terms of love for Christ. Just let the least matter come up and he will immediately think of himself, and Christ and His principles are not considered.

Here is a member of a church and something happens there that he does not like. He becomes angry. He quits going to church and withholds his gifts. Does he love Christ? No. Does He love Christ's Church? No. He is thinking only of himself; he is not seeking first the kingdom of God and His righteousness.

Here is one who is sick for five days. No one at the church knows about it, so no one from the church visits him. Self rises up, he feels neglected, he becomes angry. Is this Christlike? Here is one who hears a bit of gossip about someone. He doesn't check to see if it is true, he simply sends it on its way to hurt one who may be perfectly innocent. That is not Christ-like. That is why I say that Christ and His principles mean so little to the average church member.

What is the motive behind your relationship to Christ? Let me illustrate. Here is a young woman whose father is worth a hundred million dollars. Three young men come courting her. Let us hear what they have to say. The first young man says, "I am courting her because of her money. I don't want to be poor all of my life, I want to be a millionaire." The second young man says, "I have a heart condition and I must quit work. If I married her I wouldn't have to work." But the third young man says, "I am not courting her because of her money, I love her for herself. If she lost every penny I would still want to marry her. I love her enough to die for her." Now you know which one of the three really loves her.

Let us now turn to the spiritual realm and listen to God as He looks down upon some of our church members. He says, "Some of them are following Me simply for what they can get out of it. They want the blessings of earth and they want to go to heaven at the end of the way. They were baptized and joined the Church in the hope of getting these things." Then He would say, "Some are following Me because they are afraid of hell. They hoped that by being baptized and joining the Church they would miss hell." Then He would say, "But some are following Me because of their pure love for my Son who died on the cross. They didn't turn to Me just to gain heaven and escape hell. They really love Me and they love My Son." Oh, friends, we ought to love Him for Himself and we ought to express that love daily by living for Him and serving Him.

A ship sailed westward out of the Golden Gate some years ago. Two days out an American met a fine Chinese gentleman and said to him, "Have you come in touch with anything of the Christian religion in America?" "Yes," replied the Chinese, "I have a Bible that a missionary on board gave me as we were leaving San Francisco. I have been reading it for the past two days." Then the American asked, "What do you think of the Christian religion?" "It is fine, it is better than Confucianism." "Are you going home as a Christian then?", asked the American. "No," said the Chinese, "the Christian religion is too high for me. I could not live up to it. I will go home as a Confucianist."

The voyage was a very stormy one and on the last day

out the American again met the Chinese and said to him, "So, you're going home as a Confucianist?" "No," replied the Chinese, "I have given my heart to Christ right here on the ship and I am going home as a Christian." "Why," asked the American, "I thought you said the Christian religion was too high for you." "Yes," said the Chinese, "but I have seen it in action in a man's life right here on the ship." "Tell me about it," said the American.

"You remember the missionary who gave me the Bible. Well, I have gotten up at midnight and gone down to look upon the poor sick people in the steerage. I saw that missionary down there nursing those people and ministering to their needs. I saw him caring for a baby while the baby's mother got some rest. I saw him sitting in a good seat on deck and I saw him give up that seat to a woman and her sick child. I have seen the Christian religion really lived out in a man's life, so I am going home to be a Christian." That missionary, by his life and love, was seeking first the kingdom of God.

VI. The Promise in the Text

"All these things shall be added unto you" – all that you need. God keeps His promises and He will keep this one. Be all that you ought to be, do all that you ought to do, not just to get these things but because you love Christ. Then God will add all these things to you.

We need to put first things first. I believe it was Dr. Roy Angell who told this story. Some years ago a preacher accepted a call to a country church. On the first Sunday night he rode to church in his buggy. While he was preaching some mischievous boys changed his buggy wheels. They put the high wheels up front and the low wheels behind, just opposite to their natural position. The old preacher drove a mile to a deacon's house after church to spend the night, but the going was hard. The next morning the farmer deacon found the preacher out in front of the house, looking down the road. "What are you looking for?", asked the deacon. "I'm looking for that steep hill between here and the church." "There's no hill there," said the deacon. "There must be," said the preacher, "my horse had a hard pull last night and I was riding on my neck all the way."

They then went out to the barn and saw how the wheels had been changed on the buggy. "There's your trouble," said the deacon. They had a good laugh about it, then the deacon said, "Parson, there's a sermon for you. When you get things in front that belong behind and things behind that belong in front, you'll go through life having a hard time."

That's the trouble with so many Christians today. Jesus belongs up front in one's life and He is often put behind. If you put Him where He belongs life will always be smoother and better. Heaven is waiting for you if you are a Christian, and everything you need here will be added to you if you'll put Him first.

What do you want to do when you get to heaven? First, I want to fall down at Jesus' feet and thank Him for saving me and bringing me safely home. I don't know if I'll see the Father and the Holy Spirit as separate persons from Christ. I rather imagine that we'll see the Godhead embodied in the person of Christ. But if it's the other way I will want to thank God for giving me His Son and the Holy Spirit for convicting me and pointing me to the cross. Then I will want to see my Father and mother and loved ones and friends who went on before me. Then I'll want to greet the souls who have been saved under my ministry along the way. Then I'll want to see all the great saints who have lived on the earth and have served the Lord so well.

There are many great things waiting for us out there in heaven. But we must live here a little longer until He calls us to be with Him. And in the meantime we must remember to seek first the kingdom of God and His righteousness. If we do He will bless us and give us all we need.

On the island of Leyte during World War II a young sergeant was fighting for his life. Fifteen slugs had entered one of his legs and it had to be amputated. When he regained consciousness the doctor gave him a tag with a California woman's name on it. He said to the sergeant, "This woman's blood saved your life." The soldier was shipped back to the West Coast and one night that woman's phone rang. A man said to her, "You gave your blood to the Red Cross and it saved a young man's life. He is here at the USO station tonight and he wants to see you." The woman hurried down and when she met the sergeant they threw their arms around each other. The young man thanked her and wept tears of appreciation for the life-giving blood she had given him.

Oh, someday you and I are going to meet the Man who gave His blood for us and saved us from our sin. In the meantime what are you doing for Him? Let's put Him first, so we'll not be ashamed when we meet Him. I want to be all in this world that I ought to be, I want to do all that I ought to do for Jesus. I want to be like Him and to have His Spirit. Won't you join me in that dedication?

"But seek ye first the kingdom of God, and his righteousness, and all these things shall be added unto you."

6

THE WAY OF TRANSGRESSORS

Proverbs 13:15

Some time ago I was visiting some patients in a convalescent home, and a nurse said to me, "I want you to meet Mrs. Stine. She is an inspiration to us all." I went back to a little room and there on the bed lay a tiny woman, twisted with arthritis. When I went over to her bed she looked up and smiled. Then for several minutes she talked to me about the goodness of God and the happiness she enjoyed. "How long have you been here in this home"?, I asked her. And she answered, "Fifteen years." Think of it! Fifteen years in bed, never knowing a minute without pain, so helpless that someone else had to lift the food to her mouth. Yet she could smile and talk about God's goodness and her happiness.

Some people would be inclined to say, "It isn't fair. Why does God allow her to suffer like this?" But she doesn't complain, she just smiles and trusts God and patiently awaits the day when He will give her a perfect body.

The best Christians often suffer greatly, but their hearts are full of hope. However, the Bible tells us that "the way of transgressors is hard." They may fare well for a while, but there is nothing in the future for them but the tragedy of eternal suffering. The sinner, the unsaved man, has no hope. His happiness lasts but a little while.

I. The Way of the Sinner is the Way of Bitterness

A man starts out in sin, expecting to derive great sweetness from that sin. But soon the sweetness turns to bitterness and he finds that sin never permanently satisfies. Solomon learned this lesson. He reached out into all kinds of sin; he tried everything under the sun. Finally he cried out, "There's nothing to it, it's all vanity and vexation of spirit." Then he gives some advice to young people, "Remember God and serve Him while you are young, for the day is coming when you will find no pleasure in earthly things." Yes, you can indulge in sinful things and soon the zest will be gone, but you can follow Christ and find the pathway growing sweeter and sweeter until the perfect day.

A man in Canada had a problem. His house was on the highway just outside the garbage collection area. The garbage trucks didn't come out far enough to pick up his garbage, so he hit on a novel idea. He took the table scraps, put them in a box, tied them up in an attractive package and set the package out by the side of the road. He then looked out the window and saw a car approaching. The man in the car saw the package, stopped the car and got out. He looked around to see that no one was watching, picked up the package, got back into his car and sped away.

Now you can imagine how surprised this man was when he opened the package farther down the road and found nothing but table scraps and garbage. That is a picture of a sinner. He sees something so desirable that he steals the forbidden fruit, only to find emptiness and bitterness when sin is finished.

In New Jersey a lovely young woman went to a tailor's

shop to have a dress mended. After the tailor had finished the job the young woman gave him a big hug of appreciation. He enjoyed the sweet fragrance of her perfume and the touch of her soft arms around his neck. But when she had gone, he discovered that his billfold containing $60.00 was missing. That sweet hug cost him $60 of hard-earned money. That also is a picture of sin. It is sweet for a little while but bitter in the end.

A man got off the bus in our city with $900 in his pocket. Another man was friendly to him and offered to show him around. Soon another friendly man joined them. They went into a bar and began to drink. Before the evening was over this man had "passed out" and the two "friendly" men were gone with his $900. So a man starts out in sin, thinking the devil is his friend. But he soon finds out that the devil has robbed him and that sin brings only bitterness.

"Oh," says some young person, "I'm going to live it up. I'm going to get all the pleasure I can out of life." But one day he finds out that sin pays off only in remorse and misery and unhappiness. During World War I a popular song said, "Pack up your troubles in your old kit bag and smile, smile, smile." That kind of philosophy would tell us that all we need to be happy is to smile and forget your troubles. But I have heard that the man who wrote that song, committed suicide. It takes more than a smile to help one along life's rugged way – it takes Christ in the heart.

A boy in Massachusetts climbed up on a high electric tower. He accidentally came in contact with some live wires and was burned so badly that both legs had to be amputated. A patrolman saw him dangling on a crossbar, so he called the electric company and asked them to cut off the power, so he could bring the boy down. As they reached the ground the boy kept moaning over and over, "Why did I do it? Why did I do it?" And many a sinner, when sin pays off, must cry, "Why did I do it, why did I do it?"

II. The Way of the Sinner is the Way of Slavery

A man starts out playing with sin, then he goes too far and soon finds himself enslaved. When you go fishing you hide the hook with the bait. In like manner the devil lures us on, hiding the hook under the most attractive bait, but he catches us at last.

A certain preacher visited a man in the hospital. The man had spilled some acid on his trousers in the shop where he worked. That night he noticed a tiny red spot on his leg, but he thought nothing of it. Later the spot grew larger. He went to the company doctor, who said it was nothing serious, and who gave him some salve to rub on the spot. But it got worse and worse and he was taken to the hospital. And five days after the preacher visited the man, he stood at the head of a casket and tried to comfort a grieving widow and children. Sin is like that. It starts small, but gradually spreads until it enslaves us in a deadly bondage.

In my years as a pastor I have seen many fine men and women who were living good lives. Then they started drinking. They didn't mean to go too far, they just wanted to be sociable and agreeable. But they went deeper and deeper until sin had them in its grip. All the pleas of loved ones did no good, all the advice of their pastor was in vain, all the treatments and medicine failed. Sin had enslaved them and life became miserable for them.

III. The Way of the Sinner is the Way of Hardness of Heart

A man hears the Gospel and the Holy Spirit convicts him

of his sin and his need of a Saviour. His eyes fill with tears, his emotions become soft and tender . . . but he goes on in sin and the day comes when his heart becomes so hard that he never sheds a tear, he never feels the need of spiritual help. The greatest preachers may preach to him, the sweetest singers may sing, but he is completely unmoved.

Some psychologists have made some experiments with frogs. They learned that if you put a frog in a bucket of hot water, he would immediately sense that it was too hot for comfort and would jump out. But then they would put a frog in a pot of cold water over a slow fire and he would stay there. The water would warm up so gradually that the frog wouldn't realize the change, and soon he would be boiled to death. It is like that with a sinner. He doesn't jump off the deep end to begin with; he plays with sin and goes on and on until he has lost all spiritual feeling and his heart becomes hardened against all gospel truth.

One winter night a man walked into a church to get out of the cold. An usher graciously showed him to a seat. It was a few minutes before the service began, so the usher sat down by the man and told him the story of the three crosses. He told him how Jesus had died on the central cross, while one thief was saved when he called upon Christ and the other one died in his sin. Then the usher told the man that he, himself, had been a thief and how Christ had saved him and that he was now a respected member of that church. Instead of being moved by this testimony, the foolish stranger said in smart-aleck tones, "And mister, you know who I am? I am that other thief. I have lived without Christ and I will die without Him." And he rushed out of the church into the night.

Go back twenty or thirty years. There may have been a

time when that man had a tender heart and when he would gladly have received the message of salvation. But he had gone on and on until his heart was hardened to every good thing.

IV. The Way of the Sinner is the Way of Death

Paul said that "the wages of sin is death" (Romans 6:28). James said that "sin, when it is finished, bringeth forth death" (James 1:15). Isn't it strange that men will follow those things that lead only to death and destruction?

Roland Hill, the English preacher, saw a herd of hogs follow a man to the slaughterhouse where they were all killed. He asked the man how he managed to get the hogs to follow him. The man said, "I carry a basket of beans with me and I drop a few as I go along and the hogs follow the trail of beans, eating their way to the slaughterhouse." Satan entices men to sin and eternal death in the same way.

Now sin doesn't have to be big to lead to death. Many people think they are safe if they don't steal or murder or commit adultery. But little sins often grow until they bring death. A boy in Wisconsin murdered his aunt, crushing her skull with a hammer. When asked why he killed her in a burst of temper, he said it was because she nagged him about little things, such as washing his dirty hands.

Yes, sin brings death, death to happiness, death to peace, death to the soul. "The soul that sinneth, it shall die" (Ezekiel 18:4).

V. The Way of the Sinner is the Way of Judgment

Many people who live without Christ today act as if they will never have to give an account of their lives to a great God. Oh, how foolish they are! They can go ahead now and live in their sin and unbelief and God will not bother them. But when they come to the end of the way they are going to come face to face with a holy and righteous God. He knows all about them; He has a complete record of all they have done and said and thought in this life. In that day they will stand helpless before Him; they will be without excuse. Then, as the Bible says, they will cry out for the rocks and mountains to fall upon them and hide them from the face of Him who sits upon the judgment throne.

You may go ahead in your sin, but remember this, God is waiting for you out there. "Be sure your sin will find you out" (Numbers 32:23). Three men walked down a city street one day, and a street photographer snapped a picture of them. One of the men was so incensed that he smashed the camera and beat up the photographer. But the film in the camera was unharmed, so the photographer developed the picture and gave a copy of it to the police. The man who committed the crime was easily identified, was arrested and sentenced. No, you don't get away with sin. You may avoid its consequences today and tomorrow and all the year through, but some day it will catch up with you and punishment will come.

Now, what is the remedy for sin? There is only one, "the blood of Jesus Christ his Son cleanseth us from all sin" (I John 1:7). Come to Him with all your sin, confess that sin to Him. He will cleanse, He will forgive, He will even forget your sin. The chorus of a hymn says:

> But this one thing I know,
> That when the crimson flow
> Dropped to the earth below,
> It fell on me.

Yes, Jesus died to save you from sin. Won't you let Him save you today? Won't you let Him wash away your sin?

Won't you let Him make you ready for life, for death, for the judgment? He stands at the door and knocks. He says, "Let me into your heart. I'll take your sin away, I'll fill your heart with peace, I'll take you home to heaven." What will be your response to His loving invitation?

7

I DREAMED I WAS SENTENCED TO DIE IN THE ELECTRIC CHAIR

John 3:18

Some time ago I had a most peculiar dream. It was one of those dreams from which you awake with a great deal of relief. I dreamed that I had been condemned to die in the electric chair. I was eating my last meal, my family had gathered around me, and we were all very sad. I tried to recall what I had done. It seems that I had knocked a man in the head and he had died, but I could not remember any of the details. This was the day of my execution; I had just a little while longer to live.

I went into another room (in the dream) and tried to cheer up my family. I told them about my will and my insurance and tried to set things in order. But every time my loved ones looked at me, they began to weep. I looked out of the window and saw the sheriff coming for me. He had some handcuffs in his hand and I thought. "That's silly, I am not trying to get away." Right at that moment I woke up, and what a relief!

As I lay there after my dream I began to think of John 3:18, "He that believeth on him is not condemned: but he that believeth not is condemned already, because he hath not believed in the name of the only begotten Son of God." This verse tells us that millions of people are condemned to die a much worse death than the one I dreamed about. I asked God to give me a message out of this dream experience and several thoughts and Bible texts began to run through my mind. So I got out of bed, secured a note book, and began to get up a sermon based on this text in John 3:18.

I. Dreams in the Bible

1. *Jacob's dream.* He had left home to escape the wrath of his brother, Esau, whom he had swindled. On the first night out he slept on the ground, with a stone for his pillow. That night in a dream he saw a ladder reaching from heaven to earth. Angels were going up and down the ladder and God stood just above it. He said to Jacob, "I am the Lord thy God, I will be with thee and keep thee. I will give this land to you and your descendants and your seed will be like the dust of the earth in number." When Jacob awoke he made a promise to God that he would follow Him and serve Him and always give Him a tenth of his income.

2. *Joseph's dream.* He had two dreams and in each of them he saw himself exalted to a high place and above his many brothers. His dreams came true. After much trouble and distress he was lifted up to be the man next to the king in Egypt, and in this position he saved his brothers and their families.

3. *Solomon's dream.* He had just become the king after David's death and of course he felt a peculiar sense of inadequacy. In the dream God appeared to him and asked him what he wanted God to give him. And in a marvelous spirit of humility Solomon said, "I am but a little child, give me wisdom to rule rightly." God was pleased with

this answer and told Solomon that He would give him not only wisdom but also riches and honor. God kept that promise, even as He keeps all promises, and Solomon became the wisest and the richest and the most famous man of his day.

4. *Joseph's (Mary's husband) dream.* Mary and Joseph were engaged to be married when Mary was found to be with child of the Holy Spirit. She was to bring God's Son into the world. But Joseph did not know this, so he prepared to put Mary away privately to save her from public shame. Then in a dream God told him to go ahead and marry Mary. Later in another dream he was told to take Mary and the baby Jesus into Egypt. Still later in a dream he was told to return home.

5. *Pilate's wife's dream.* When Jesus was brought before Pilate, Pilate's wife tugged at his sleeve and said to him, "Don't have anything to do with harming this just Man. I have suffered many things this night in a dream because of Him." But Pilate brushed the warning aside and delivered Jesus over to be crucified.

6. *Cornelius' and Peter's dreams.* These two dreams caused Peter to go and preach to Cornelius and win him to Christ. From this event Christianity branched out to include the Gentiles.

7. *Paul's dream.* Paul saw a man from Macedonia in a dream. The man was saying, "Come over into Macedonia and help us." Thus guided, he brought the Gospel to Europe. There are many other dreams recorded in the Bible.

But someone will say, "God revealed His will to men in dreams in those days. Why doesn't He do that today?" It is because we have the Bible and the Holy Spirit to guide us today. God reveals His will in this way. A man reads his Bible and looks for the leading of the Holy Spirit, and thus he finds God's will for his life.

There are some things about which we don't have to seek God's will through prayer and waiting on God, for they are already revealed so definitely in God's Word. The Bible tells us not to steal or kill. We don't have to ask if these things are wrong or not, the answer is there in the Bible. I asked a man one time if he didn't think he ought to give some of his income to the church and the Lord, and he said, "I'll have to pray about it." But there's no need to pray about what God has told us directly to do, we are just to go ahead and do it.

There are some things, however, that are not directly revealed in His Word, and that's where the Holy Spirit does His work. Jesus said that the Spirit would guide us into all truth. So when a decision is to be made, we are to pray and ask the Holy Spirit to guide us. One of my friends gave up a very fine pastorate to go to a pioneer area and take over a small, struggling church, at a great reduction in salary. But he did it because he felt that the Holy Spirit was leading him.

God uses various methods for different times. Once he used dreams to convey messages, now He uses the Bible and the Holy Spirit.

II. In This Dream it Seems I Had Killed A Man

Yes, I plead guilty, I did kill a Man. You helped me to kill Him. His name was Jesus Christ, God's Son from heaven. How did we kill Him? We killed Him with our sins. If we had never sinned, God's heart would never have been broken. If He had never come to this sinful world, He would never have been lied about, He would never have suffered and died on Calvary's cross. But our sins nailed Him to the tree.

We often hear the question, "Who killed Jesus Christ?" We know that the Jewish leaders condemned Him and cried out for His death. We know that Pilate officially turned Him over to the soldiers. We know that the soldiers carried out their orders and nailed Him to the cross. This was all part of the big plan. But primarily you and I are the real murderers, for by our sin we sent Him to the cross. These others things would not have happened if we had not been guilty of sin.

> I saw One hanging on a tree
> In agony and blood,
> He fixed His languid eyes on me,
> As near His cross I stood.
>
> Sure never till my latest breath,
> Shall I forget that look,
> It seemed to charge me with his death,
> Tho' not a word He spoke.

He had a right to charge you and me with His death. We were guilty sinners. We committed the blackest crime in the world, the crime of crucifying the sinless Son of God. On the day that I dreamed I was to die, I could only vaguely remember the crime I had committed. So it is that the story of the cross becomes so familiar to us that we become hardened to it. Sin becomes such a habit that we never feel any conviction for it.

A person commits a certain sin for the first time and it upsets him so that he can hardly stand himself. He says, "I never thought I would do such a thing. I'll never do it again." But in a few days the tempter comes again and he falls again. This time he doesn't feel so badly. So he keeps on until after a while he commits this sin and has absolutely no compunction of conscience because of it.

What makes a man a drunkard? It is his first drink. If it had not been for that he would never have become a drunkard. What makes a man an adulterer? It is his first impure act. What makes a man a thief? It is his first dishonest act. Oh, if we could just avoid that first sin!

But there is hope for us when we have sinned. In I John 2:1 God says that we are not to sin, but "if any man sin, we have an advocate with the Father, Jesus Christ the righteous." An advocate is one who pleads for you. If you have sinned, come to Jesus. Confess your sin, turn away from it. He'll plead for you at the bar of heaven and His pleas are always heard. Your sin will be forgiven.

III. In the Dream I Saw That I Was Condemned

When a man murders another man he is tried before a jury. If he is found guilty, the judge passes sentence on him, in many cases condemning him to death. But the Bible tells us that every one of us is condemned, not just to a physical death, but to eternal death. Let us look again at the text, "He that believeth on him is not condemned: but he that believeth not is condemned already, because he hath not believed in the name of the only begotten Son of God" (John 3:18).

Why are men condemned to eternal death? Is it because they have lied or stolen or cheated or killed or lived impure lives? No, it is because they have not believed on the Son of God. All these sins spring from and grow out of that unbelief.

Go with me to your state prison. We walk down death row with the warden and he says, "That man in cell number seven is to die at 6 o'clock next Friday morning in the electric chair." I stop at cell number seven, put my hands up on the bar, and look into the eyes of a condemned man. It gives me a strange, creepy feeling. Here is a man strong and alive and active. But on Friday morning, in two minutes' time, his life will be snuffed out and he'll soon be cold in death.

But let me tell you something more awful. A man without Christ is already condemned to die. You look at him on the street, in his home, at work or maybe here in the church. He is a criminal for he has rejected Christ, his only hope. He is condemned to die and suffer eternally in hell. The Bible calls this "the second death." It is truly just that. That is why we ought to witness to others about Christ. This is why we ought to live good Christian lives before them. That is why we ought to bring them to church to hear the Gospel. They are lost and only Christ can save them.

Now when a judge condemns a man, it may be months before the sentence is carried out. I can imagine such a man in his prison cell on death row. On the calendar he marks off the days he has left to live. He counts them down, 29, 28, 27 and so on. Every day brings him closer to his doom. So God has condemned every man who has rejected Christ, although it may be months or years before the sentence is carried out.

What does the Bible say about that day? Let us look at some related Scriptures.

"The wicked shall be turned into hell, and all the nations that forget God" (Psalm 9:17).

"In flaming fire taking vengeance on them that know not God, and that obey not the gospel of our Lord Jesus Christ: who shall be punished with everlasting destruction from the presence of the Lord, and from the glory of his power" (II Thessalonians 1:8, 9).

"Then shall he say also unto them on the left hand, Depart from me, ye cursed, into everlasting fire, prepared for the devil and his angels" (Matthew 25:41).

"And whosoever was not found written in the book of life was cast into the lake of fire" (Revelation 20:15).

"And shall be tormented day and night forever and ever" (Revelation 20:10).

Sinner, count your days. Every day is bringing you closer and closer to the fatal day of judgment. Your time may be shorter than you think. But you can escape damnation, you can get out from under condemnation. This can be done if you will repent of your sins and turn to the Lord Jesus Christ for salvation. He says, "Him that cometh to me, I will in no wise cast out" (John 6:37). And John says, "As many as received him, to them gave he power to become the sons of God" (John 1:12).

An evangelist was holding a meeting in Florida. During the invitation time he went down and spoke to an old man about his soul. "Son," said the old man, "I heard the Gospel before you were born." The preacher said, "Then you've been rejecting Christ a long time, haven't you?" The old man then said, "I'll be saved before I die, but I am not ready yet." The preacher pled with him to come to Christ right then, but he said, "Not tonight, I'll be saved some time." The next morning the preacher heard that the old man had died in his sleep that night, died without Christ.

God says, "He that, being often reproved hardeneth his neck, shall suddenly be destroyed, and that without remedy," (Proverbs 29:1). Oh, condemned man, come now, let the Saviour pardon you and lift your condemnation.

IV. In My Dream I Said, "Maybe I Did Kill A Man, But I Wouldn't Do It Now, Feeling As I Do"

That's the way a man feels after Christ comes in to his heart. "If any man be in Christ, he is a new creature" (II Corinthians 5:17). When you are made over by Christ, sin doesn't come as easily as it once did. You don't have as strong a desire to sin as you did before.

One day I had a meal in the home of a man who belongs to a group that doesn't believe in eternal security. He didn't believe in the Biblical doctrine of "once saved always saved." He said, "If I am saved and can't be lost, then I can go out and kill a man and still go to heaven." I answered, "That's just the point. If you have been saved, you will not want to kill anyone. Christ has made you over and given you a new heart, a heart that will keep you from wanting to do such things." I am not saying that a Christian is perfect and will never commit sin, but I do say that he won't have the tendency toward sin that he formerly had. He will want to say with Paul, "I am dead to sin."

A man was saved and joined the church and became very faithful. One day he came to his pastor in great distress. He said, "I forgot myself, cursed a man and wanted to kill him. But I am certainly sorry. I wonder if I am a Christian after all." The pastor asked, "In the old days were you ever sorry when you sinned?" "Oh, no," he answered, "but it breaks my heart now." Then the pastor wisely said, "That proves you are a Christian, the fact that you now worry about your sins." He was right, with Christ in your heart you don't have the old desire to sin.

Oh, yes, we often slip up, but God gives us relief at that point. "If we confess our sins, he is faithful and just to forgive us our sins, and to cleanse us from all unrighteousness" (I John 1:9). We are not to confess our sins to a man, to a priest, but to God Himself. We remember that David was a man after God's own heart, yet he sinned grievously. But then he repented genuinely and was forgiven gloriously. Then he sang the praises of God when relief came. That is the pattern for us to follow when we have sinned.

I remember also that in my dream I was not broken up, but my family was in sorrow and I had to comfort them. It's that way with a Christian. No sorrow faces him when he faces death, the sorrow is borne by the loved ones who are left behind. The dying Christian can say, "A wonderful thing is happening to me for I am going to be with Jesus and to enjoy heaven. You must stay here, but I'll be a million times better off. To live is Christ and to die is gain."

V. In My Dream I Tried to Set My House In Order

I showed my family my will, insurance policy and other valuable papers. A man ought to do these things. He ought to make out a will and make provisions for the future of his family. I Timothy 5:8 says that a man who doesn't provide for his household is worse than an infidel.

When the time came for Hezekiah to die, the Lord sent him a message, "Set thine house in order; for thou shalt die and not live" (II Kings 20:1). That is God's message to every man. If the Lord tarries, we shall all go through the experience of death. But more important than any material preparation we must make is our spiritual preparation. The prophet of old shouted out, "Prepare to meet thy God." Have you made that preparation? You may have sufficient insurance to care for your family, you may have your home paid for and your will in good order. But that is not enough if you are not ready to meet God. Those things will not count at the Judgment Bar.

And some of you Christians need to set your house in

order. You must meet Christ at the Judgment Seat and account for all you have done here and have all your works judged. If you are living for the world, you are not ready. If you don't put Him and His Church first in your life, you are not ready. If you are spending everything on self and not giving God His part, you are not ready. If you are cold and indifferent and neglectful toward spiritual matters, you are not ready. But you can get ready to meet Him by cleaning up your life and becoming active for God.

Years ago you came to Christ, you repented of your sin and trusted Him as your Saviour. According to Romans 8:1, your condemnation passed away. But the Christian life doesn't end there. You have a life to live for Him who gave His life for you. I know we won't be perfect this side of heaven. We shall make mistakes and fail and sin and run ahead of the Lord. But we ought to do our best for the Saviour. Simple, common gratitude ought to impel us to do that. Christian, set your house in order, resolve that from now until the end of the way Christ and His cause will come first.

Oh, friend without Christ, you are condemned already. The wrath of God is waiting to fall on you. Set your spiritual house in order. A rabbi said to his students, "You ought to repent the day before you die." "But we don't know when we'll die," said a student. "Then," said the wise man, "You ought to repent now." I would say the same thing to you.

"Boast not thyself of to-morrow; for thou knowest not what a day may bring forth" (Proverbs 27:1). Now is the only time you have, so come to Jesus now. One day the heavy hand of death will be laid on your shoulder. The great Executioner will say, "Your hour has come, follow me." Oh, what if you are not ready to go? What if you let the days go by without giving your heart to Christ? What if you put off the matter of your salvation until it's too late? Unsaved man, set your house in order.

A young man who found Christ in a Victory Center in Chicago told this experience. He had been a paratrooper in World War II. One day he and nine other paratroopers were to make their first jump from a plane. He was the third in line. When the moment arrived for the jump the first man stepped out bravely, his parachute opened up and he floated to safety. But the second man lost his courage and stood to one side. So this boy summoned up all his courage, stepped out and floated down to the earth. As he descended he heard a loud explosion above him. He looked up and saw that the plane had exploded and was falling apart. Every man on board died, including the boy who had his chance and missed it.

If you are without Christ, your hesitation can be as fatal as that boy's indecision. But the door of mercy is open, Christ is waiting to save you. Don't wait until it's too late. Come to Jesus now and be saved forever.

8

THE THREE HARDEST WORDS TO SAY

I John 1:8-10

Someone has said that the three sweetest words in the English language are, "I love you." The three hardest words to say are, "I have sinned." It is hard to get most people to say, "I was wrong." It is harder still to get them to say, "I have sinned." John, in writing to Christians, tells us that we have sinned and those who say they have no sin are liars. Then he says that "If we confess our sins, he is faithful and just to forgive us our sins, and to cleanse us from all unrighteousness" (I John 1:9).

Now while this text applies primarily to Christians, it can be applied also to all who sin. If a lost man confesses his sin and trusts Christ, he is forgiven. If a saved man confesses his sins, he is forgiven. Of course, along with the confession there comes the idea of turning away from sin. If a man says, "O God, I have sinned," and continues in that sin, no forgiveness is given him.

I. We Do Have Sins to Confess

1. *The Bible says so.* "For all have sinned, and come short of the glory of God" (Romans 3:23).

"For there is not a just man upon earth, that doeth good, and sinneth not" (Ecclesiastes 7:20).

"You . . . were dead in trespasses and sins" (Ephesians 2:1).

"The heart is deceitful above all things, and desperately wicked" (Jeremiah 17:9).

Adam and Eve were the first people on earth and they sinned. Everyone who has lived since their day has gone down into sin. Sin begins at birth, it operates in childhood, it grows as the years continue, it follows us down to the grave. Go and find the best man in the world, the man who has climbed closest to God, and that man must say, "I know there is sin in me."

2. *Our conscience tells us that we have sinned.* Everyone has a conscience which rings out like a bell, telling us that we have sinned. A young woman in a certain community went astray. She had a baby born out of wedlock. She wanted to get rid of the baby, so she killed it and buried it in the woods. When she was arrested the good women of the community came and tried to help her. She would listen to them for awhile, then she would cry out, "But I can't get away from the baby's cry." Conscience won't let us forget our sins.

II. Some Bible Confessions of Sin

1. *Pharaoh, the hardened sinner.* God's people were in bondage in Egypt, so God sent Moses to Pharaoh to demand that they be set free. But Pharaoh laughed at Moses and said, "Who is God? I am the king. I have all power, get out of my palace." Moses left, but God will have His way. He sent plague after plague upon Egypt and its people.

Still Pharaoh would not let the people go. Finally the greatest tragedy of all struck. The first-born in every Egyptian home died during the night. Even Pharaoh's son, the crown prince, was not spared. And what did Pharaoh do? He sent quickly for Moses and said to him, "I have sinned, I give up, God has won, the Israelites can go." So Moses gathered the thousands of God's people and led them out of Egypt and toward the Promised Land.

But what happened? Pharaoh changed his mind. His confession of sin meant nothing at all. He gathered his army and went charging out after Moses and the Israelites. You know the story. The people of God crossed over the Red Sea on dry land, while Pharaoh and all of his hosts were drowned.

That's the case of a hardened sinner. Under some pressure he says, "I have sinned, I'll give up. I'll live for God." But when the trouble blows over he goes back to his sin.

Dr. Truett tells about a Christian doctor coming into his church one Wednesday night just as the preacher was about to pronounce the benediction. The doctor said, "Wait just a minute, pastor. Down the street there is a man who is critically ill. I don't think he has many more hours to live. Tonight he asked me if this were not the night when God's people came together for prayer. When I told him that it was, he said, 'Go to the church and tell them to pray for me. Tell them to promise God for me that if He will let me get well, I will come to church, I will confess Christ as my Saviour. I will live for God.' Pastor, will you please pray and make that promise for this man?" The pastor said, "Yes, we will all pray for him." And he led the congregation in a fervent prayer, making the sick man's solemn promise to God.

When the doctor went back to the man's house the next day, he found him greatly improved. Then in a few days he was out of bed and soon he was back at work·again. One

Saturday Dr. Truett met the man on the street and said to him, "You'll be coming to God's house tomorrow, won't you?" And the man replied, "I can't come tomorrow, preacher, when I was sick I fell behind in my work. I must work tomorrow." "But," said the preacher, "don't forget that vow you made to God and how God saved you from death. You need to come to church and carry out your part of the bargain." "Oh, yes," said the man, "I was in a tight place then and I had to do something. But don't worry, I'll be there at church one of these Sundays."

The weeks went by and this man never came to church. Then one morning when Dr. Truett picked up his morning paper, he saw a headline telling of this man's sudden death. The day before he had been at the railroad station, talking and laughing with a group of friends. Suddenly his hand went up to his heart, he fell upon the floor and was dead before the ambulance arrived. The great preacher said that the only text that filled his mind for weeks was, "To-day if ye will hear his voice, harden not your heart" (Psalm 95: 7, 8).

Have you made some high and holy vow to God? Have you, in some great hour, promised to live for Him? Have you, by an open grave, sworn in your heart that you would follow Christ? Then don't forget your pledge. Come to Him and He will save you and forgive your sins.

2. *Balaam, the wavering sinner.* Balaam one day saw a good man die. "Lord," he said, "Let me die the death of the righteous, and let my last end be like his" (Numbers 23:10). But he soon forgot this worthwhile desire and went over altogether on the side of God's enemies.

This is a picture of the wavering sinner. Under the stress of a high emotional hour he says, "I will do thus and so," but his vow is soon forgotten as he goes back to the things of the world. I have seen men mightily moved by a sermon. I have seen the Holy Spirit get hold of them until they shook like a leaf. Then they went out into the world, forgot the sermon, put off the matter of their salvation and went on toward death.

3. *Achan, the last minute sinner.* Joshua's army, under God, had been victorious and triumphant wherever they fought. Then one day they went up against the little town of Ai and were driven back, dismally defeated. Joshua knew that there was some reason for this defeat, so he fell on his face before God and asked Him the age-old question, "Why?" God said, "There is sin in the camp. Get it out and victory will come." So Joshua searched the camp and found the guilty man. Achan had stolen some Babylonish gold and garments and hidden them in his tent, going against the commandment of God. The penalty for this crime was death, so Achan and his family were taken out and stoned to death. As he was led away he cried out, "I have sinned, I have sinned."

Achan is the type of the man who, when he is facing death, remembers his sins and cries out to God. Now some of these deathbed confessions may be genuine, but I am afraid that the majority of them are brought on by fear. The lesson to be learned here is simply that men are not to put off their salvation until they are almost staring into the face of God's judgment. When you are dying you may not have the intelligence to repent of your sin and trust Christ. So do it now.

The Bible gives us only one case of a man who was saved just before he died. This was the thief on the cross. You will never be in exactly the position he was. And remember that he had probably never seen Jesus before that day, he had never had a chance to be saved. But you have had many chances. So while your wits are about you, while you know just what you are doing, you ought to come to Christ.

Another thing about Achan. His family died with him. That is the tragedy of sin, for it not only destroys the sinner, it also hurts others. "No man liveth unto himself." We carry someone else to heaven or to hell. A son or daughter in hell can point his or her finger at a father or mother and say, "I am here because of you. You never went to church, you never prayed, you never read the Bible. I followed you and now I am lost forever." Oh, the tragedy of living without Christ and taking others to hell with you!

4. *The Prodigal Son – the repentant Sinner.* After his sinful fling in the far country, we find him in a hogpen many miles from home. Let us look at the four steps that brought him to his father's house.

(1) *He came to himself.* This simply means that he came to his senses, he saw himself as he was, he saw things in the right light. He thought of his home and all the things he had once enjoyed. He saw what a fool he had been to leave it all.

This man did some thinking. That's what so many people need to do today. They need to think of God's goodness and they need to think of their sin. They need to think of what happens to a man who leaves God out of his life. A sinner needs to come to his senses.

(2) *He was filled with sorrow.* He said, "I will go back and tell my father that I have sinned and am no more worthy to be called his son. I will go back and take a servant's place." That's the way a man must feel before he can be saved. He must say from his heart, "Lord, I don't deserve thy salvation. I am not worthy of it and I know it.

But I know it's better to be a servant in God's house than to be a slave in the far country."

(3) *He made a good resolution.* He said, "I will arise and go." Oh, it's a great thing when a man can say, "I'll do it, I'll live for Christ." The battle is half-won when you make up your mind about the matter.

Someone asked Alexander the great how he conquered the world and he answered, "By making up my mind and not delaying." Why not make up your mind about Christ, resolving that He will be the Lord of your life?

(4) *He put his resolutions into action.* It was not enough for him to feel, he must act. He arose and came to his father. You know what happened. His father saw him a long way off and ran to meet him. He kissed him and loved him and said, "Bring the best robe and put it on him, bring the family ring for his finger. Kill the fatted calf and let's make merry. My son is home, my son who was dead is alive again, my son who was lost is found."

You know, God is waiting to do the same thing for you. Think of your needs, think of your sins, think of death that's coming, think of eternity. Then arise, leave your sin and come to Jesus. He is waiting to save you.

III. Christ Forgives Our Sins

Christian, are you a backslider? Have you grown cold and indifferent? Are you neglecting your Christian duties? Then you need to come to Christ for forgiveness. Come back to Him and His service and find again the joy of your salvation.

Now am I speaking to one who is lost, to one who has never put his or her trust in Christ? He is just as ready to receive you as the prodigal's father was to receive him. Why do you go on without Christ? You don't know what tomorrow will bring, so why neglect this matter another minute? If this were your last day to live on this earth, you know you would go out into eternity without God and without hope.

Hebrews 9:27 says, "It is appointed unto men once to die, but after this the judgment." Without Christ you are not ready for that appointment.

Years ago just outside one of our cities a great train was wrecked. All of the passengers in one of the pullman cars were killed. With the exception of one young man, they lived in this same city. The body of the young man could not be identified. The caskets were taken to the city hall, where a funeral service was to be held for all of them. Men, women and children came and filed by the caskets to take one long last look into the faces of their friends and loved ones. And wives and mothers and daughters and sisters came and bent over to plant the last kiss on the face of their beloved.

But nobody kissed the stranger's face for no one knew him. Finally a dear little woman walked by the caskets. She saw the women kissing their loved ones good-by, but noted that no one stopped at the stranger's casket. So she went to that casket leaned over and said, "I'll kiss him once for his mother's sake." And she gave him her kiss.

Oh, my friends, far more quickly than that does Christ want to give you His kiss of forgiveness and salvation. That kiss will be yours right now if you will only turn away from your sin and trust Him as your Saviour and Lord.

9

THE KISSES OF THE BIBLE

Kisses are mentioned several times in the Bible. Today they are customary in most countries. A kiss is usually between members of the opposite sex. However, in France and other countries men kiss each other on the cheek. In Hawaii a lei, a circle of flowers, is placed around the neck and then the cheek kiss is given.

In this message I will not speak of kisses from a sensuous standpoint, but from a spiritual standpoint. In the Bible every kiss except that of Judas is crowned with beauty, sentiment and spirituality. Let us look at some of these kisses and see if we can draw from them a spiritual lesson and a blessing for our own hearts.

I. The Kiss of Welcome

"And it came to pass, when Laban heard the tidings of Jacob, his sister's son, that he ran to meet him, and embraced him, and kissed him, and brought him to his house. And he told Laban all these things" (Genesis 29:13).

Jacob had just run away from home. He had cheated his brother Esau of his birthright and his blessing. He was afraid that Esau would seek him out and kill him, so his mother, who aided him in the deception, told him to go to her old home in Haran. She also influenced her husband, Isaac, to advise him to do the same thing.

So Jacob went to Haran and finally met Rachel, who is to play such a big part in his life, at the watering place for the flocks. He told her who he was and she ran home to tell Laban, her father. When Laban heard this news he ran out to the well and embraced Jacob, giving him a kiss of welcome. He said, "Let this be your home now, we are your kinspeople, everything we have is yours." He really didn't mean it in exactly that way, for he forced Jacob to work fourteen years for Rachel.

Now look at the spiritual lessons here. When a sinner comes home to Christ, the Saviour gives him a kiss of welcome. Oh, how glad is Jesus when someone is saved! "Joy shall be in heaven over one sinner that repenteth" (Luke 15:7). God is not a God of folded arms. He cares for the sinner, He yearns over him, He longs for his salvation. Then when that sinner does turn to Him, He welcomes him with the kiss of forgiveness.

Then when a sinner comes to Christ a new relationship is established. When Laban kissed Jacob, he was simply recognizing the relationship that existed between them. So we become the "sons of God" when we come to Christ. We hear much these days about "the Fatherhood of God." The inference is made that all men, regardless of their condition, are the sons of God. This is not true, for that relationship is established only when by faith we come to trust in the Lord Jesus Christ. God created all men, but He is the Father only of those who believe. "But as many as received him, to them gave he power to become the sons of God, even to them that believe on his name" (John 1:12).

Then when a sinner comes to Christ, all that Christ has

is his. Paul tells us that we are "heirs of God, and joint-heirs with Christ" (Romans 8:17). My, what an inheritance! All that the Father has is ours in Christ. Here is a poor man who is struggling to make a living. Then a rich man says to him, "Come and live in my home and all that I have will be yours." That's what God says to us. We were poor lost sinners; we needed salvation, peace of heart and forgiveness of sin. We would be fools to refuse all that God gives us, for He offers us everything good in two worlds.

In one of my pastorates there was a couple who had three boys, but no girls. Then they adopted a little red-haired baby. She was a darling and all the family loved her. She became the boss in the family, and all that they had was hers. So when we are adopted into God's family, all that He has is ours. He gives us the kiss of welcome.

II. The Kiss of Restored Fellowship

"Moreover, he [Joseph] kissed all his brethren, and wept upon them: and after that his brethren talked with him" (Genesis 45:15). Joseph was a dreamer, the acknowledged favorite of his father, and it was only natural that his brothers would be jealous of him. So one day they seized him and sold him into slavery in Egypt, then they reported to their father, Jacob, that Joseph had been killed by a wild beast. Joseph endured many hardships in Egypt, but the time came when he was elevated to the place of prime minister of the country, a position next to that of the ruler, Pharaoh.

Twenty-two years went by and a famine arose in all lands, but there was grain in Egypt because of the good work of Joseph. So Jacob sent his other sons to Egypt to buy grain. None of them knew that Joseph was alive and certainly none of them knew about the high position he held in Egypt. Joseph, who recognized his brothers, put them to several tests. Finally, he revealed himself to them as their brother. Instead of hating them or killing them as he could have done, he fell upon their necks and kissed them. Surely he must have been the most Christ-like man in the Old Testament.

Now let us learn some spiritual lessons here. First, our fellowship with Jesus is often broken. Our relationship is not altered, for we are still the children of God. After David's great sin he did not say, "Give me back my salvation." He said, "Restore unto me the joy of thy salvation." If you are God's child before you sin, you are God's child after you sin. But your fellowship with God is broken by your sin.

Hundreds of real Christians have lost the joy of their salvation. Sometimes this comes about because of sin, sometimes it is because they have neglected their simple Christian duties and obligations. It is only natural that the backsliding Christian doesn't feel close to God anymore. But fellowship with God can be restored if you return to God in penitence, even as David did.

Then we learn here the lesson of forgiveness. If any man ever had a right to hold a grudge, that man was Joseph. But in spite of the shameful way his brothers had treated him, he forgave them from his heart. In Philippians 2:5 we read, "Let this mind be in you, which was also in Christ Jesus." If we have the mind of Christ we will have a forgiving spirit. Even as they put Him to death He prayed, "Father, forgive them; for they know not what they do" (Luke 23:34).

But someone says, "I can forgive but I cannot forget." Such an attitude is of Satan. When we bury the hatchet we must not leave the handle sticking out. It has been said that "forgiveness is the odor of flowers trampled upon." When people hurt you and you forgive them, a sweet fragrance rises up to bless them and you. They can't help but be impressed with your brand of Christianity. Unforgiveness adds to our burden and takes the sweetness out of our religion.

Why not try this? When something comes up between you and someone else, go to them and say, "I want to do the right thing. If I have hurt you in any way, I want you to forgive me. Let us be friends." Oh, the devil may jump up and tell you not to do this, but you should beat him down and say, "I am a Christian and I am going to do the right thing, no matter what the cost." The other party may not respond, but you will know that you have done your part. You have cleansed the hatred out of your own heart and that will be a blessing.

III. The Kiss of Love

"And as soon as the lad was gone, David arose out of a place toward the south, and fell on his face to the ground, and bowed himself three times; and they kissed one another and wept one with another" (I Samuel 20:41).

King Saul was jealous of young David, because David was becoming too popular. But Saul's son, Jonathan, and David loved one another. So when Saul plotted to kill David, Jonathan ran to tell him of his danger. When they met out in the field they fell into each other's arms and wept and kissed one another.

Here is another great spiritual lesson for us. As David found a friend, so can we find our best friend in Jesus Christ. He is indeed a friend who "sticketh closer than a brother."

What a friend we have in Jesus,
All our sins and griefs to bear!
What a privilege to carry
Ev'rything to God in prayer!
O what peace we often forfeit,
O what needless pain we bear,
All because we do not carry
Ev'rything to God in prayer.

Have we trials and temptations?
Is there trouble anywhere?
We should never be discouraged –
Take it to the Lord in prayer.
Can we find a friend so faithful
Who will all our sorrows share?
Jesus knows our ev'ry weakness –
Take it to the Lord in prayer.

Are we weak and heavy laden,
Cumbered with a load of care?
Precious Saviour, still our refuge –
Take it to the Lord in prayer.
Do thy friends despise, forsake you?
Take it to the Lord in prayer;
In His arms He'll take and shield thee –
Thou wilt find a solace there.

Dr. J. M. Gray was serving as president of the Moody Bible Institute. He became ill and planned to go abroad for his health. But a few days before his ship was scheduled to sail, he had an attack of sickness and missed the boat. He was greatly disappointed and wondered why he had to wait. Then he heard that the ship on which he was to have sailed was sunk at sea. Dr. Gray then felt somehow that God was showing him his love in this disappointment.

Often we say, "If God loves me, why did He allow this to happen to me?" Maybe He did it because He does love us. Sometimes this is God's loving way of saving us from something worse. He is a friend who never fails us. "Having loved His own, He loves them to the end."

IV. The Kiss of Gratitude

"And all the people went over Jordan. And when the king was come over, the king kissed Barzillai, and blessed him; and he returned unto his own place" (II Samuel 19: 39).

There came a time when David was in trouble and when he fled to Mahanaim. An old man there by the name of Barzillai cared for him, hid him from his enemies and supplied all his needs. When the time came for him to leave, David wanted to express his gratitude to the old man, so he said, "Come with me to Jerusalem and I will take care of you the rest of your life." But Barzillai was eighty years of age and didn't want to leave his old homeplace. So he declined David's offer. Then they walked together as far as the Jordan and when the time came to say "good-by," David embraced the old man and planted a kiss of gratitude upon his cheek.

The spiritual lesson here is that Christians ought always to be careful to express their gratitude. If someone has shown you a kindness, let him feel your gratitude and appreciation.

In the state of Georgia, just after the Civil War, an old soldier was running for an elective office against a younger man. One day the two candidates spoke from the same platform. The old soldier was not much of a speaker, the young man was a real orator. He swept the crowd with his oratory and brought them to their feet in applause. When the young man sat down a friend of the old soldier rushed up to the platform and lifted the empty sleeve of the old soldier. "Ladies and gentlemen," he cried, "behold the results of Pickett's charge at Gettysburg." Then he pointed to the empty sleeve and the scar on the old soldier's face, and urged them to remember these things on election day. A few days later the people expressed their gratitude by electing the old soldier to the public office.

But I am thinking of another One who was wounded. He went to Calvary and died for us. See the wounds in His hands, His feet, His head, His side. He is most worthy of our gratitude, and we can best express that gratitude by giving Him our very best from day to day.

V. The Kiss of Betrayal

"And forthwith he came to Jesus, and said, Hail, Master; and kissed him" (Matthew 26:49).

Judas was the man who gave the kiss of betrayal. He had previously bargained with the enemies of Christ, so when the Master came out from His place of prayer Judas kissed Him, thus identifying Him to His enemies, who then took Him away to be crucified.

What is the spiritual lesson here? Men still betray the Lord Jesus, not with a kiss, but with the sins we commit, the words we say, the thoughts we think!

Some time ago a man died in one of our state penitentiaries. He had been there for thirty years. A railroad was being built and they wanted to buy the right of way across this man's land. He refused to sell. The case was taken to the courts and the railroad won. They paid the man a good sum for the right of way, but anger rankled in his heart. So one night, after the railroad had been built, he dynamited the track, wrecked the train and caused the death of a number of people. He was sent to prison, where he remained thirty years until he died. It took him thirty minutes to place the dynamite and thirty years to reap the harvest.

It took Judas only a few minutes to betray Christ, but he has been paying for it ever since. We, too, pay the price when we betray Christ.

VI. The Kiss of Approval

"Every man shall kiss his lips that giveth a right answer" (Proverbs 24:26). In Solomon's days in the Orient, approval was expressed by a kiss. If someone did the right thing or gave the right answer, they received this kiss of approval.

And here is the spiritual lesson for us in this text. If we live for Jesus, some day we shall receive His kiss of approval, some day He will say to us, "Well done, thou good and faithful servant." The road of life may be long and hard and it wouldn't be worth the struggle unless there was something better waiting for us. But the toils of the road will seem nothing when we get to the end of the way.

> Friends will be there I have loved long ago,
> Joy like a river around me will flow;
> Yet, just a smile from my Saviour, I know,
> Will through the ages be glory for me.

VII. The Kiss of Reconciliation

"And he arose, and came to his father. But when he was yet a great way off, his father saw him, and had compassion, and ran, and fell on his neck, and kissed him" (Luke 15: 20).

I don't have to tell you the old familiar story of the Prodigal Son, for you are well acquainted with it. The sweetest part of the story comes when the boy's father rushes out to meet him and gives him the kiss of reconciliation.

What is the spiritual lesson here? If you are in the far country of sin you will never be satisfied. You will be able to eat only the husks that Satan provides. There will be no happiness in your life, no peace in your soul. But God is waiting to give you His kiss of reconciliation. He is waiting to forgive you and to provide a feast for you and finally take you home in glory.

Just as a Scotch minister was about to enter his pulpit, he heard that one of his members was dying. He rushed over to the man's house and said to him, "Sandy, I have just four minutes to give you, tell me how you were converted." And Sandy said, "Oh, Jesus just came and said to me, 'Sandy, I'll exchange with you.' I asked Him what He meant and He said, 'You give me all your sin and I'll give you My salvation.' And I gave Him all my years of sin; I gave Him my sinful heart, and in return He gave me His salvation and His righteousness and heaven."

That's the plan of salvation plainly put. You come with all of your sin, turn it all over to Jesus. In return He will give you eternal life. So come, come to Jesus, come as you are and let Him give you the kiss of reconciliation and everlasting life.

> Just as I am, without one plea
> But that Thy blood was shed for me,
> And that Thou bidd'st me come to Thee,
> O Lamb of God, I come! I come!

10

THE ASSURANCE OF OUR SALVATION

I John 5:13

Blessed assurance, Jesus is mine!
O what a foretaste of glory divine!
Heir of salvation, purchase of God,
Born of His spirit, washed in His blood.

Fanny Crosby wrote this wonderful song that has been sung around the world. Now when you know that Jesus is indeed yours, when you know you've been saved, you can sing the chorus:

This is my story, this is my song,
Praising my Saviour all the day long;
This is my story, this is my song,
Praising my Saviour all the day long.

Some Christians have no assurance of salvation. Some believe they can be saved today and lost tomorrow. They must be very unhappy people. I would be miserable if I continually lived in fear that at any moment I might slide off the track to heaven and land on the road to hell. I don't believe God wants us to be filled with doubts and fears. Satan is the author of doubt. If he succeeds in getting us to doubt our salvation, he robs us of all spiritual power.

A preacher asked a boy, "Does Satan ever tell you that you are not saved?" "Yes," replied the boy. "Then what do you tell him?", the preacher asked. "I tell him it's none of his business," answered the boy. But too many of us listen to the devil.

God wants us to be saved. We know that. And He also wants us to know it. He knows if a Christian can say from his heart, "Yes, I am saved and I know it," he will have more power than a doubter.

I. Why Do Some People Lack the Assurance of Their Salvation?

1. *They lack assurance because of false ideas about the Christian life.* They say, "I am not perfect, I don't live as I should, so I'm afraid I haven't been saved." Christians ought to live better lives, we know that. But we are not necessarily lost because of our imperfections. The best Christians are not perfect.

The test comes when you fall into sin. What do you do next? Do you remain in sin or do you seek to rise up and put your hands anew in the nail-pierced hands of Jesus? Years ago I heard an evangelist use this illustration. He said that if a pig found a mud puddle he would wallow in it. You might drive him out of that hole, but when he came to the next mud puddle, he would jump right in again. That's the nature of a pig. But suppose a sheep fell into that mud puddle. He would get out as quickly as possible, then he would carefully avoid the next mud hole. That's the nature of a sheep.

Now that's the difference between a real Christian and a non-Christian. The sinner falls into sin. Something might scare him out of that sin, but when another temptation confronts him, he embraces the sin. He wallows again in the mudhole of sin. But when a real Christian sins he is not happy. He climbs out of that mudhole, confesses his sin to God and takes a tighter grip on the Lord Jesus. Then he shies away from the next temptation that assails him.

After Judas had committed his great sin, he showed signs of remorse, but absolutely no signs of repentance. If he had been a genuine Christian he would have sought Jesus and fallen at His feet in repentance. And Jesus would have forgiven him. Now when Simon Peter sinned he was not happy, he was miserable. He wept his heart out in repentance and came back to Jesus. We know he was a genuine Christian. When David, a man after God's own heart, committed his great sin, he was heavily burdened about it until he came back to God and cried out for mercy and forgiveness.

Christians are not perfect, and they often fall by the wayside. But that does not mean that they are bound for hell.

2. *They lack assurance because they lack the consciousness of a definite Christian experience.* In some of the great city rescue missions a man will often stand up and say, "On a certain night in a certain month of a certain year I was saved right here on this spot."

Now it isn't always like that with all people. While some of us cannot point to the day and hour and minute and spot where we were saved, we do know that God's Spirit witnesses with ours, telling us that we are the children of God.

When I was in the seminary I served as pastor of a small church in East Texas. Arthur Giles was a deacon and a faithful member of that church. I heard the story of how he had been saved. One night, during a revival meeting, he came under deep conviction and saw himself as a lost sinner. That night he stayed behind to talk with the preacher.

Before long he was rejoicing in his new-born salvation. He mounted his horse and rode toward home, shouting his praise to God all along the way. One of the neighbors who heard him, said, "Arthur Giles got religion tonight." Many years went by before I became his pastor, but on one occasion he said to me, "When Satan tempts me and tries to make me doubt my salvation, I go back in my experience to that night and I receive fresh assurance of my salvation."

But many genuine Christians have never had such an experience – they cannot point to the very minute when they were saved. But deep down in their hearts they know they are new creatures in Christ Jesus.

3. *They lack assurance because of their simple neglect of their Christian duties.* They have become indifferent in their service to Christ and Satan has led them down the pathway of doubt.

The Bible is on the table, but they never open it. They never go to some sacred spot to pour out their hearts to God. They seemingly care nothing for the church, everything else comes before it. They take God's tithe and use it for themselves. They know they are not doing the things God would have them to do. No wonder the doubts arise.

A young man was converted and joined the church where Dr. George W. Truett was the pastor. He was for a time faithful to every service and every responsibility. Then he gradually drifted away from the church. One day, filled with Satanic doubts, he came to Dr. Truett and requested that his name be taken off the church roll. He said, "I never should have joined the church. I am afraid I was not saved when I went forward. I want my name dropped from the church membership roll." Dr. Truett was very patient with the young man. He said, "We'll take your name off the roll, but first I want you to do one thing for me. I want you to go to see an old couple who are members of our church, then come back to see me." The boy said, "All right, at least I can do that."

That night, just before the evening church service, the young man fairly ran into the pastor's study. "Dr. Truett," he said, "Don't take my name off the roll. Everything is all right. I know now that I am a child of God and from now on He and His Church will have my best." "What happened this afternoon?", asked the great pastor. "I went to see that dear old couple and we had a wonderful time together. They are poor and they are sick, but they kept on talking about God's goodness to them. Just before I left they asked me to read a chapter in the Bible and have a prayer with them. I did this and when I arose from my knees they were shouting. And pastor, I am afraid I shouted a little bit, too."

The young man was back on the right track and all the doubts were gone. If some of you would get busy for God, maybe you would have fewer doubts.

4. *They lack assurance because of their worldliness.* Maybe you've been running with a worldly crowd. You have yielded to their pressures and the devil's temptations. You have done those things that worldlings do. No wonder your mind is filled with doubt. You will never find assurance until you repent of your sinful worldliness and come back to a spiritual life.

David could say, "The Lord is my shepherd." He had assurance at that time. But when sin came in he lost the joy and the assurance of his salvation. Then when he came back to God the old sweet faith and confidence filled his heart and he could say, "Blessed is he whose transgression is forgiven, whose sin is covered" (Psalm 32:1).

II. The Dangers of Doubt

1. *Doubt robs us of peace and joy.* Christians ought to be happy, in fact, they are the only people who have a right to be happy. Paul tells us to "rejoice always." We have something to rejoice over, but we can't rejoice if we don't know we have it.

Can you say, "Floods of joy o'er my soul like the sea billows roll"? Can you say, "I have the peace that passeth all understanding"? Not if your heart is full of doubts.

Some years ago I held a meeting in a church in Georgia. A fire station was located just across the street. The fire captain, who was not a Christian, came to several of the revival services. One night the pastor and I talked and prayed with the captain in the pastor's study. That night, on his knees, that man gave his heart to Christ. The next morning he had to lead the fight against a disastrous warehouse fire. Several hours later he came over to the church to tell us about it. He said, "I used to be afraid of such fires, afraid that the walls would cave in on me or that the burning embers would fall on me. But I had no fear today, for I realized that for the first time I had a wonderful Friend with me." Yes, he had Christ, he had peace, and fear was cast out.

2. *Doubt prevents us from doing effective work for Christ.* How can we point others to Christ if we are not sure of Him ourselves.

An out-of-town preacher was conducting a revival in a certain small-town church. On his first day there he stopped a little boy on the street and asked the boy to point out the way to the post office. Then he said to the boy, "Come to our meeting at the church and I'll show you the way to heaven." Then the boy said, "How can you show me the way to heaven if you don't even know the way to the post office?"

If you try to win a man to Christ and there are doubts in your own heart, your witness cannot be very effective. If you have to say, "I hope I'm a Christian, but I'm not sure," your Christian work will not be very successful.

3. *Doubt dishonors God.* God says in His Word, "Him that cometh to me I will in no wise cast out." He says, "He that believeth on the Son hath everlasting life." You say, "I have done that, but I don't know whether I am saved or not." You are dishonoring God, for you are saying that He does not keep His promises. Doubt dishonors God.

4. *Doubt makes us fear death.* As you think of death and the judgment to come, if you are not sure you are saved, you are filled with fear. The man who really is sure of his salvation has no fear of death and the life beyond.

General Stonewall Jackson said as he lay dying, "I am just going to cross over the river and rest beneath the shade trees on the other side." Dwight L. Moody said, "Earth is receding, heaven is descending and I am going home." Paul said, "I have fought a good fight, I have finished my course, I have kept the faith: Henceforth there is laid up for me a crown of righteousness, which the Lord, the righteous judge, shall give me at that day: and not to me only, but unto all them also that love his appearing" (II Timothy 4:7, 8). These men had the assurance of salvation, so there was no fear of death in them.

A woman was on a boat going from Buffalo to Cleveland. A storm arose and all the other passengers were afraid, but she was very calm. She said, "It's like this. I had two daughters. One died and is in heaven, the other one lives in Cleveland. If the boat goes down I'll see my daughter in heaven, if not I'll see the one in Cleveland. It doesn't matter which one." She had assurance and there was no fear of death.

III. The Grounds of Our Christian Assurance

1. *We can't base our assurance on our feelings.* We are sometimes up and sometimes down. Some days we are on the mountain top, other days we are in the valley of despondency. Some days we feel that we are very near to God, other days we feel that we are near the pit of perdition. We can't base our assurance on our feelings.

2. *We can't base our assurance on our works.* In one of my early pastorates I preached on salvation by grace, stating that our works had nothing to do with our salvation. In my congregation there was a woman who was quite faithful, but who was rather self-righteous. After I had preached this particular sermon, she said, "Well, I've done lots for the Lord, and I know that has something to do with my salvation." She was wrong. It is not what we do that saves us, but what Christ has done.

> Could my tears forever flow,
> Could my zeal no languor know,
> These for sin could not atone –
> Thou must save, and thou alone:
> In my hand no price I bring,
> Simply to Thy cross I cling.

3. *We must base our assurance on the Word of God.* "The Word of God abideth forever." A man says to me, "Do this for me and I'll give you one hundred dollars." Now he may keep that promise and he may not, for he is human. But when God says, "Believe on the Lord Jesus Christ and thou shalt be saved," I know He will do it, for He never breaks a promise. If you meet the conditions of salvation as laid down in the Bible, you can know that you are His and He is yours.

When Evangelist J. Wilbur Chapman was a student, there came a time when he began to doubt his salvation. He went to see Mr. Moody about it and Moody quoted John 5:24 to him, "He that heareth my word, and believeth on Him that sent me, hath everlasting life, and shall not come into condemnation; but is passed from death unto life." Then Mr. Moody asked, "Do you believe in Christ?" "Yes," Chapman answered. "Then are you saved?" Chapman said, "I don't know." "Young man," thundered Moody, "whom are you doubting?" And like a flash the truth dawned on Chapman. He had been doubting Christ and the Word of God.

4. *Other Biblical grounds of assurance.*

(1) *Joyful obedience.* "And hereby we do know that we know him, if we keep his commandments" (I John 2:3). If you are a Christian you will want to obey Christ, you will want to do all He commands His followers to do.

In a meeting that Dr. J. M. Gray was holding, a twelve-year old girl made her profession of faith. "When were you saved?", the preacher asked her. She replied, "I was saved last Sunday but I wasn't sure of it until Friday." "How did you know then?" She said, "I told my mother." Yes, if one is saved he will want to obey the command to confess Christ before the world. Those who will not make this confession can never be sure of their salvation.

(2) *Christian love.* "We know that we have passed from death unto life, because we love the brethren" (I John 3:14). If you don't love people, how can you say that you are a child of God?

If we love people, we like to associate with them. Yet multitudes of church members absent themselves from the services in God's house Sunday after Sunday. They prefer the company of the world. A man who can go everywhere else but to church is certainly not right with God.

(3) *The witness of the Spirit.* "The Spirit itself beareth witness with our spirit, that we are the children of God" (Romans 8:16). This is something that no one can explain, it must be experienced. But if you are a child of God, there is something inside that makes your spirit long to reach out and contact God's Spirit.

F B. Meyer was a great preacher of London. In his last illness he wrote these words to a friend, "They tell me that I have only a few days to live. It may be that before this letter reaches you, I shall have entered the palace of the King. Don't bother to write, I'll see you in the morning." The great man of God had the assurance.

A little boy was gloriously converted. Later his mother made a profession of faith in Christ. But it was hard for her to understand that one is saved by simple faith. One night she heard a sermon on John 5:24 and went home rejoicing in Christ. But the next morning all the doubts had come back. She said, "Son, the feeling is gone." Then he ran and got the Bible and found this wonderful text of assurance. He showed it to her and said, "Mother, it's still in the Bible, you are all right."

Yes, all the glorious promises are still in the Bible. So, if you have repented of your sin, if you have carried out the instructions in His Word, you can be assured that you are saved.

God keeps His Word. You and I have a hope that is steadfast and sure.

11

THE BEST THINGS IN THE WORLD

Philippians 1:8-11

The church at Philippi seemed to be Paul's favorite. It was probably the first Christian church to be established in Europe. We remember that Paul's first converts there were the Philippian jailer and his family and Lydia and her household. They surely were members of this church at Philippi. As Paul traveled over the world I can imagine that Lydia would write him and say, "Preacher, I'm so glad you came to our prayer meeting by the riverside that Sabbath Day, for that was when you told me about the saving power of the Lord Jesus." And the jailer would write, "Preacher, I'm so glad you were in my jail the night the earthquake came, so you could tell me that I could be saved by trusting in the Lord Jesus Christ."

Yes, I am sure that Paul loved the Philippian church. In the letter that he wrote to them there was not even one word of rebuke. But he tells them that he is praying for them and that he wants them to give their thought and approval to the "things that are excellent." Now the things that are excellent are the best things in the world, they are the things that excel, they are the things that surpass all other things.

For instance, we believe that our country excels other countries, so we say it is excellent. We believe that our churches, or our schools, or our climate excel, so we say they are excellent. And surely we can call our Saviour excellent for He excels by a million miles all others who have ever lived. Now the Christian has some excellent things. Let us consider some of them.

I. We Have Experienced An Excellent Birth

Not all of us can say that our first birth was excellent. We may have been born in a very poor place under very obscure circumstances. Even Jesus the Son of God was born in a stable. But if He is our Saviour we can say that our second birth was an excellent one.

We first learn about the second birth as we hear Jesus talking to Nicodemus. This fine man, this Jewish leader, this member of the Sanhedrin, came to Jesus one night and poured out his soul. And Jesus looked deep into this hungry-hearted man and said, "Nicodemus, you must be born again. Except you are born again you cannot enter into the kingdom of God." Nicodemus was like so many of us, he thought only of the earthly side of things, so he said, "I don't get it. Can a man enter the second time into his mother's womb and be born?" And Jesus said, "Wait a minute, Nicodemus, I'm not talking about a physical birth, but a spiritual birth. You must be born again spiritually to be saved."

Then Jesus went on to tell Nicodemus how he could be born again. "And as Moses lifted up the serpent in the wilderness, even so must the Son of man be lifted up: That whosoever believeth in him should not perish, but have eternal life" (John 3:14, 15). "For God so loved the world, that he gave his only begotten Son, that whosoever believeth in him should not perish, but have everlasting life" (John 3:16). "He that believeth on him is not condemned: but he that believeth not is condemned already, because he hath not believed in the name of the only begotten Son of God" (John 3:18).

Now Jesus puts the emphasis here on believing on Him. And believing on Him means receiving Him, trusting Him, clinging to Him for salvation. If you have done that you have been born again, born into the kingdom of God. "But as many as received him, to them gave he power to become the sons of God, even to them that believe on his name" (John 1:12).

You may receive high degrees from the greatest universities, but the best degree you can ever receive is God's "B.A." degree, God's "born again" degree. Nothing in the world can take the place of the new birth, Reformation, culture, church membership, good works cannot save you. No man ever gets on the road that leads to heaven until he has been born again, until he has had an inner experience with Christ.

One of the false teachings of today is that there are many roads that lead to God and heaven. One man pictures heaven as a beautiful palace standing in a delightful garden. There are many roads leading to the palace and many pilgrims are walking on these roads. Some of the roads are rough and rocky, some are smooth and flowerstrewn. But all these roads lead to the palace. This is a pretty picture, but it is not true. There is only one way to God, one way to heaven and that is through Jesus Christ – not through a church or a ritual or a man-made institution, but through Jesus Christ. Jesus said, "I am the way, the truth, and the life: no man cometh unto the Father, but by me" (John 14:6).

Oh, if you have had this excellent birth, you are on the right road, the only road that ends up in heaven.

II. We Have an Excellent Nature

All of us are born with a sinful nature. Then when we are saved God gives us a new nature, a spiritual nature. He doesn't take away the old nature, and that's why we always have a fight going on within us. It is the carnal fighting against the spiritual, the good fighting against the bad, the old nature fighting against the new nature.

Here is the way it works. Before you are saved, when a temptation comes along, you go right ahead and commit the sin without thinking much about whether it's right or wrong. Then after you are saved, when the same temptation arises, the old nature says, "Go ahead, you know you've always enjoyed it." But the new nature says, "You're a Christian now, you must center your thoughts on higher things." Then the battle begins. Some people lose the battle, because they give in to the old nature. Some win, because they say, "From now on Christ is my Master. Get thee behind me, Satan."

Some time ago I sat in a man's outer office, waiting to see him. His secretary was busy at her desk in this outer office. The phone rang and she answered. I could hear her saying, "Thank you. Yes, I'll be glad to come to your party." Then there was a moment of silence when, evidently, the person on the other end of the line was talking. Then the secretary said, "Oh, I'm sorry, if it's going to be that kind of a party I cannot come." She then expressed her thanks and hung up the phone. Being curious about the matter (as most preachers would be) I went over and asked her why she had so readily accepted the invitation and then had turned it down. She said, "There was a time when I went to parties like that, but no more. Some time ago I found Christ as my Saviour and now I am teaching a class of girls in the Sunday school, so I don't go to cocktail parties any more." As I listened to her I knew I had found someone who was winning the battle.

We are definitely told in the Bible that spiritual things are not understood by the carnal mind. One time I heard a preacher on the street, talking to an unsaved man about the Holy Spirit. The man stood there with a blank stare on his face. He didn't know what the preacher was talking about. But the born-again person knows the Holy Spirit, for He lives in the Christian's heart, comforting, guiding, convicting, blessing.

Now I do not mean to say that anyone lives a perfect life, simply because he has this new spiritual nature. But I do say that a man lives a better life after he has received the new nature. He can say, "The things I once hated I now love, and the things I once loved I now hate."

III. We Have Excellent Clothing

I have read of people who possessed 100 suits of clothes. I am afraid, however, that many of them do not have a spiritual wardrobe. What is this spiritual clothing which every Christian has? It is the righteousness of Christ. We are not righteous, we are not perfectly right. But when we come to Jesus He clothes us with His righteousness. We are sinners in our natural state, but when we come to Him He wraps His robe of righteousness around us, so that when we face God He will not see our sin. He will see us just as righteous as His Son, Jesus Christ.

Jesus pictures the Prodigal Son away from home, down and out, feeding pigs, clothed in rags. But look at him as he goes home. He's dirty, he's ragged, he's emaciated. The dogs bark at him and the children stone him. But as he tops a familiar hill an old man sees him, he runs to meet him, he hugs him and kisses him. He doesn't wait for the boy to clean up. He says to his servants, "Bring the best robe and put it on him, we're going to have a great feast." And it's that way when we come to Jesus. He covers all our sins; He puts His robe of righteousness around us; He gives us the best He has.

Did you know that you can't enter heaven unless you have this robe on? Jesus tells about a man who went to a wedding feast. Now in order to get into the feast, everyone had to wear a wedding garment. They didn't have to buy these garments, they were furnished free of charge, they were given out at the door. But this particular man said, "I don't want to put on that suit. I'll get in all right." He went into the banquet hall, but when they saw that he didn't have on a wedding garment, they threw him out.

Today God says, "In order for you to get to heaven you must wear a robe of righteousness." And Jesus says, "I have a robe ready for you. It is just your size; it is free for the asking." But men spurn that offer, they try to get to heaven on their own merits. Let me tell you that they will be cast out into hell.

The Bible says that without holiness no man can see the Lord. But it is not our holiness. It is the holiness or righteousness of Christ which is imputed to us when we are saved. This is the garment He gives us, this is the righteousness which is put to our credit on the records of heaven when we are born again.

Most of us have traded certain things. As children we traded marbles or a knife, as men we have traded cars and houses. But the best trade any man can ever make is when he comes to the foot of the cross and trades his sin for the righteousness of Christ. The old garment of sin is traded for the new garment of His holiness.

IV. We Have Excellent Attendants

Some wealthy people have many servants to look after them – a chauffer to drive the car, a butler to open the door and serve the meals, an upstairs maid, a downstairs maid, a cook and a valet. But the richest man on earth without Christ doesn't have the attendants that we have. The Book of Hebrews tells us that the angels are ministering spirits, sent forth to minister to God's people. God made the angels, not only to do His bidding, but to serve us.

We are living in an age of crass materialism. Not many people believe in angels today. But God is still using them to take care of His people. You were riding in a car one day and you were forced to pull over to avoid a horrible accident. Maybe your guardian angel caused you to do that. When I was a boy I almost put my hand down on a poisonous snake on the creek bank. But I saw the snake just in time and quickly drew back my hand. Maybe my guardian angel pulled my hand back. Maybe he said, "God wants this boy to be a preacher some day, so I must save him."

Simon Peter was arrested one day and put in prison. Sixteen soldiers were assigned to guard him and he was to be killed the next day. But God said to one of His angels, "I have some more work for Peter to do. Go down and release him and lead him out of the prison." So the angel came down and did his work so quietly that the soldiers who were chained to Peter didn't wake up. And Peter went on to do a great work for the Lord.

That has been a long time ago but God doesn't change. As He used angels then, so He uses them now. They come to us when we need them most. They are wonderful to have around.

V. We Have an Excellent Comforter

God provides for everything. He looked down over the ages and knew His people would often be lonely, that their hearts would sometimes break with sorrow. So Jesus said before He went away, "I am going to send you a comforter. He will never leave you; He will always be there in time of need." So the minute a person is saved the Holy Spirit comes to live in his heart. The dedicated Christian doesn't have to go to a psychiatrist or counselor for help. The Holy Spirit is "nearer than hands and feet and closer than breathing."

One of our preachers tells about performing the marriage ceremony for a lovely nurse and a fine young man. They were absolutely devoted to each other. The lovelight gleamed in their eyes, and they were very happy. They went away on their honeymoon and came back full of joy. They were going to begin married life in a sweet little cottage. Prospects like the rosy dawn gleamed forth for them. They were driving at night and the fog was heavy. They came around a curve and met a team of horses and it was too late to stop. The horses parted and the tongue of the wagon came through the windshield and struck the young man. He died right beside his bride. Later when the preacher talked to the bride, she said, "Pastor, I don't know what I am going to do. My mind is a perfect wilderness of confusion, but my heart is at peace."

That's what I mean when I say that we have an excellent Comforter. When troubles come, when sorrows like sea billows roll, if we know the Saviour, we have the Holy Spirit within to give us comfort.

I could say that we belong to an excellent organization, the church. I could say that we are engaged in an excellent service, the service of Christ. I could say that we enjoy excellent fellowship, that of Christian friends. But I will say just one more thing.

VI. We Have An Excellent Hope

It is the hope of seeing Jesus face to face and dwelling with Him and our loved ones and friends in heaven forevermore.

When we are young heaven doesn't mean much to us. We hear about the golden streets and the pearly gates and all of our thoughts of heaven are material thoughts. But as we grow older heaven becomes more personal, because our loved ones are crossing over one by one and joining the blood-washed throngs in glory. Then we are bound to the heavenly throne by the silver cords of memory and we long to see them again in the presence of Christ.

Often down here the road is rough and steep. There are many disappointments and heartaches here, but none in heaven. We often follow the hearse to the cemetery, but there are no graves on the hillsides of glory. We often weep bitter tears here, but God shall wipe away all of our tears up there. We often brush shoulders with sinful people down here, but then we shall have fellowship with Jesus and angels and the saints of all ages.

Do you have this excellent hope, the hope of heaven and everlasting life? On what do you base that hope? Oh, if you base your hope on your own self, your own life, your own character, your own goodness, you are standing on a false foundation. There is only one basis for a heavenly hope.

My hope is built on nothing less
Than Jesus' blood and righteousness;
I dare not trust the sweetest frame,
But wholly lean on Jesus' Name.
On Christ, the solid Rock, I stand;
All other ground is sinking sand.

Aunt Bet was a dear Christian woman who taught a class of boys in the Sunday school for many years. Years later some Christian workers approached an unsaved man, who had been in Aunt Bet's class when he was a little boy. They told him that he ought to join the church, that all he needed to do to be saved was to join the church and live a good life. But the man remembered some of Aunt Bet's teaching, so he said, "I know I ought to be in the church, but before offering myself for church membership I know I must have that something which Aunt Bet used to talk about in Sunday school."

We know what "that something" is. It is the new birth which comes from a personal experience of repentance toward God and faith in Christ as Saviour and Lord. And after you have had that experience the Lord is going to fill your life with these best things in the world that we have been thinking about.

12

THE LAUGHTER OF THE BIBLE

Ecclesiastes 3:4

The word "laughter" is mentioned thirty-eight times in the Bible. Sometimes it is born out of sunshine, sometimes it is born out of midnight darkness. Sometimes it stirs the sympathy of the angels, sometimes it makes the devils rejoice. Without claiming any originality for these thoughts I want to call to your attention five kinds of laughter mentioned in the Bible, and I shall back each type of laughter up with the scripture.

I. The Laughter of Skepticism

"Then Sarah denied, saying, I laughed not; for she was afraid. And he said, Nay; but thou didst laugh" (Genesis 18:15).

Here is the picture. Abraham and Sarah were old people and they had no children. Three guests came their way one day, one of them surely being the Old Testament manifestation of Christ Himself. In true Oriental hospitality Abraham invited them for dinner and they accepted the invitation. He ran and killed the fatted calf and told Sarah to prepare the meal. Soon they were enjoying a good meal. As they ate and talked the Lord told Abraham that they would have a son, even though he was one hundred years of age and Sarah was ninety. Sarah had been eavesdropping on the conversation and when she heard this promise of a child, she laughed in unbelief. "Why did Sarah laugh?", asked the Lord. Sarah was frightened and said, "I didn't laugh." But the Lord said, "Yes, you did laugh."

Now Sarah's skepticism and unbelief have been echoed down the ages. Men do not believe, they laugh at God and the great truths of the Bible. Yet God's Word shall stand forever, even as it did in the case of Abraham and Sarah, for in due time a son, Isaac, was born to them.

1. *Men laugh at the miracles of the Bible.* They say, "These things are contrary to the laws of nature." Well, what are the laws of nature? They are simply God's way of doing things. He made these laws and He can change them. It is your rule to ride to church, but you can change that rule if you desire. You can walk. It is your rule to enter one door, but if you so desire you can change your rule and enter another door. Well, God made the rules and laws of nature and He can change them. The sun rises in the east, but God could change the entire solar system if He so desired.

God's Word is true and faithful. The miracles in the Bible are sometimes hard for some people to accept, but they happened just as they are recorded in His Word. Men laugh and say, "These things could not have happened." But God says, "They did happen."

2. *Men laugh at the great facts of the Bible.* They read those first majestic words in the Bible, "In the beginning God created the heaven and the earth." And they laugh and say, "It was all a process of evolution." They read about Noah and the Ark and they laugh and say, "There never has been such a flood." They read about the plagues of

Egypt and they say as they laugh, "It was all jugglery and trickery." They read about the death of the first-born in Egypt and they laugh and say, "It was an epidemic that killed them." They read of how God turned back the Red Sea that the Israelites might pass over and they laugh and say, "A violent wind did it." They read about Jonah and the big fish and they laugh and say, "Impossible."

They read about Christ's virgin birth and they say as they laugh, "It could not have happened." They read of how Jesus caused the blind to see and the deaf to hear and they laugh and say, "It was due to human surgery." They read about the raising of Lazarus from the dead and they laugh and say, "Mary and Martha and Lazarus and Jesus just acted out that little drama." They read about the resurrection and laugh and say, "The disciples stole his body." They read about the judgment and they laugh and say, "That's just a vivid picture drawn by an overzealous imagination."

They may laugh, but "he who laughs last, laughs best." Some day God will laugh at their calamity. He will have the last laugh.

I believe all of the Bible. I believe that it is God's holy Word for the men of this earth. There are some who would like to tear out parts of it. They would take out the account of the creation, then Genesis would be gone. They would take out the miraculous guidance of God as He led Israel to the Holy Land, and Exodus would be gone. They would take out the divinity of Christ and the four gospels would be gone. They would throw out Revelation and Christ's final triumph and heaven would be gone. Let men tear out the divine and the miraculous, and the heart of the Bible would be gone. It would be just like any other book.

Throw the Bible aside and you have a world in darkness. There would be no comfort in sorrow, no salvation for the soul, no hope for the future. We had better hold on to the Bible, the time is coming when we will need the help that only God's Word can give us.

Go to the dock in New York and look at one of the great ocean liners as it moves out to sea. There are hundreds of rooms in the ship, state rooms to live in, dining rooms to eat in, ballrooms to dance in, decks to walk on and play on. And beneath the water lines we find the mighty machinery which pushes the ship across the ocean. You ask the question, "Who made this marvelous ship?" And the answer comes back, "No one." You ask, "Who is running the ship?" And the answer comes back, "No one." Then you know there is something wrong.

Go to the railroad station and you see a mighty locomotive there, capable of pulling a hundred cars at seventy miles per hour. The train is guided by a complex system of lights and switches. You ask the questions, "Who made this engine? Who laid the rails? Who bridged the rivers? Who runs this complex system? Who pulls the switches? Whose hand is on the throttle?" And when the answer comes back, "No one," you know something is wrong.

Go to the airport and you see a mighty jet plane there, capable of flying through the air at 600 miles an hour, carrying more than 100 passengers. You watch the plane speed down the runway and take off into the blue. Soon it is flying across the country 30,000 feet above the earth. And you ask the questions, "Who designed this mighty steel-bird? Who built her? Who flies her through the air?" And when the answer comes back, "No one," you know something is wrong.

Now look at the world. It whirls on its axis at a great speed. It is warmed by the sun 93,000,000 miles away. The sun rises and sets on time and the moon and the stars come out to illuminate and beautify the night. Day and night alternate perfectly and the four seasons follow each other in perfect order. The earth gets hot in season and cold in season. It is filled with men and animals and glorious scenery. Everything that man needs is produced on its surface and in its bowels. You ask the questions, "Who made the world? Who is running the universe?" And when the answer comes back, "No one," you say that someone has lost his reason.

We know that the Bible is true, we know that God created this marvelous universe, we know that the miracles happened just as they are recorded in God's Word. Theodore Parker laughed at these things for twenty-five years while he served as a Unitarian preacher. Then he said, "I am a failure. Socially I am an outcast, domestically I have no children, professionally I am not recognized. I laughed at true Christianity, now it laughs at me."

The laughter of skepticism is an ugly and foolish laughter. It takes away all faith and all hope.

II. The Laughter of Spiritual Exaltation

"Then was our mouth filled with laughter, and our tongue with singing" (Psalm 126:2). As the psalmist thought upon the goodness of God, it made him laugh with joy.

The redeemed soul has a right to laugh. His sins have been covered, he has God's best things in this life and in the life to come. He is on the road to heaven. But you say, "Yes, I know I am saved, I know I'm on the way to heaven, but I have so much trouble right here and now." Then listen to Paul. He says, "As sorrowful, yet always rejoicing; poor, yet making many rich; having nothing, and yet possessing all things" (II Corinthians 6:10).

A speaker in a certain rescue mission was talking to a

group of boys about heaven. Then he asked the question, "Where is heaven?" And one little fellow said, "Heaven is in our home since daddy met Jesus." He was right. If you have Jesus in your heart you have a right to be happy, and it makes others happy, too.

So, let us laugh and be happy. We are no longer on the slippery path, no longer on the way to hell. We have been saved, we have Someone to help us in time of trouble, we have Someone to take us home at the end of the way.

Christians ought to be cheerful, they ought to laugh more. If you wear a long face no one will ever see any beauty in your religion. We ought to be happy and show the world that the Lord is a better master than the devil. If you have diamonds for sale you don't hide them in a black box. If your religion has helped you, don't cover it up. Let people see that Jesus has made you happy.

During World War II, when we heard that our side had lost a battle, the news had a demoralizing effect on us. When we heard of victories won, our spirits were buoyed up. The Christian is on the winning side. Jesus is his Captain, his Leader, his Sustainer. He is going to bring us out on the victorious side. So let us laugh about it, let us be happy in Christ, let us tell the world that it's great to be a Christian.

III. The Laughter of Sinful Merriment

"For as the crackling of thorns under a pot, so is the laughter of the fool" (Ecclesiastes 7:6).

1. *The sinner's laugh is an empty one.* In the picture here we see a pot hung up, with thorns burning under the pot, making a crackling noise. The thorns flash up and then they are consumed and there is nothing left but empty silence. The sinner's laugh is like that, it is a miserable thing.

His fun never permanently satisfies, it is soon over and empty and dead.

Someone said to a dear old black man, "Would you like to be rich?" And he answered, "No, sir, all the rich men I work for never laugh." He was simply saying that the things of this world do not satisfy.

2. *The sinner's laugh soon dies out.* A certain wealthy man said, "I have all that I need to make me happy." But his laughter didn't last. The crash came and he lost his money. Now he had nothing left to make him happy, so he committed suicide.

The poorest man in the world is the man who doesn't have a Saviour. When sorrow comes there is no one to comfort him. When trouble comes there is no one to bring him through. When death comes there is no one to walk with him through the chilly waters. When judgment comes there is no one to stand for him. The sinner's laugh doesn't last.

IV. The Laughter of God's Condemnation

"He that sitteth in the heavens shall laugh" (Psalm 2:4). "I also will laugh at your calamity" (Proverbs 1:26). A man builds his life like a man building a tower. He goes ahead without any thought of God. Then there comes the time when that tower comes crashing to the ground. The God who sits in the heavens shall laugh at his calamity. Man proposes, but God disposes.

A man wants to make a million dollars, by hook or crook. So he bends every effort toward his goal, caring not for the laws of God or man. He finally has one hundred thousand dollars. Then he gathers all together in one grand move of speculation, hoping to make that million. But it's a false move and he loses all. Then it's God's time to laugh.

Rome was once a great empire, powerful and wealthy.

She ruled the world. Why did she fall into ruins? Did an earthquake destroy her capital city? Did enemy legions overthrow and defeat her armies? No, Rome was a nation who defied God. She lived in sin, lust, luxury and pleasure. And God brought her down. "He that sitteth in the heavens shall laugh."

God loves men. He wants them to repent of their sin and be saved. In His great love He sent His Son to die for lost sinners. Jesus went to Calvary and bled His life away. He gave His all. From that cross there goes out the heavenly invitation, "Look unto Me and live. With this blood I will cover your sin, I will save your soul. Look and live." But men reject that invitation, they defy God, they boast that they can get along without God. But a time of calamity will come to them, a time when the God they defied will laugh at them.

Listen to these words of God, "Because I have called, and ye refused; I have stretched out my hand, and no man regarded; But ye have set at nought all my counsel, and would none of my reproof: I also will laugh at your calamity" (Proverbs 1:24-26).

God gives men every chance to be saved now. But they disregard God, they pass Him by. Calamity will surely come to them. They will be cast into the lake of fire. God will have every right to laugh.

V. The Laughter of Eternal Triumph

"Blessed are ye that weep now: for ye shall laugh" (Luke 6:21). Heaven is a happy place. We weep here, but we shall laugh there. "Weeping may endure for a night, but joy cometh in the morning" (Psalm 30:5).

1. *It will be a laughter of congratulation.* You meet a friend here who has had an operation or been seriously ill,

and you congratulate him on his recovery. And when we meet our friends in heaven, we shall laugh and congratulate each other.

We'll say to one, "The last time I saw you, cancer was eating away your body. Now you have a new body and you'll never be sick again. Congratulations." To another we'll say, "The last time I saw you, arthritis had crippled you. Now you can run as a messenger of the king. Congratulations." To another we'll say, "The last time I saw you, you were wasting away with tuberculosis. Now you have an eternal bloom on your cheek. Congratulations." To another we'll say, "The last time I saw you, you were grappling with sin. Now you have overcome it forever. Congratulations." To another we'll say, "The last time I saw you, you were burdened with sorrow. Now you have peace and comfort. Congratulations."

2. *It will be a laughter of reunion.* Have you ever been to a family reunion? Those who have not seen each other for a year laugh as they shake hands with a loved one or throw their arms around another one.

I remember the sad wail of a sick mother as her baby was wheeled away to be buried. She cried out, "Good-by, my darling. I'll never see you again." But there will be no such cry in heaven. Mother is gone, but we'll see her again. Father and brother and sister and child, husband and wife, they are gone, but not forever. We shall see them again in that blessed, better land.

3. *It will be a laughter of forgetfulness.* We have our difficulties and our differences down here. Up there we'll forget all of these. Up there we shall all love one another.

4. *It will be a laughter of sweet memories.* We'll talk about the good times we had down here and these memories will flood over us, to make heaven ever richer and sweeter.

Here we remember the touch of a vanished hand, there we'll feel its touch again. Here we remember a voice that is stilled, there we'll hear that voice again.

5. *It will be a laughter of victory and triumph.* Satan often overcomes us here, but at last we'll gain the victory over him. He'll be in hell where he belongs and he can never tempt us again.

Wellington returned in triumph from Waterloo. Teddy Roosevelt returned in triumph from Cuba. Pershing returned in triumph from France. Eisenhower returned in triumph from Germany. They had won some great victories and they marched home in glory, leading a triumphant procession.

Oh, but how much more triumphant, how much greater will be the heavenly triumphant procession! Jesus will head the procession and we'll be with Him laughing and rejoicing, all sin and sorrow behind us, and a glorious eternity before us.

As a Christian lay dying he said, "I see the letter 'W' written all over the Skies." "What do you think it means?", someone asked. And he replied, "I think it means welcome, welcome to heaven."

Yes, soon life's little day will end and we'll be going home. Welcome will be written over the gate, over the door of our mansion, over the throne and all over heaven. So let us trust Christ and love Him and serve Him well. Then up there all our sorrow and sighing will be turned into blessed eternal laughter.